AS Psychology
Revision Guide
For The 2015
Edexcel Specification

Faye Carlisle

Introduction

About this guide

This revision guide covers Units 1 and 2. It includes descriptions of key studies, theories, treatments, example practicals and research methods. It also uses a clear system of evaluation throughout, which makes it easier to evaluate in the exam.

Edexcel Examination Structure

Unit 1 examines your knowledge of social and cognitive psychology. Unit 1 is worth 50% of the marks at AS and is assessed in an 90 minute exam.

Unit 2 examines your knowledge biological psychology and learning theories. Unit 2 is worth 50% of the marks at AS and is assessed in a 90 minute exam.

Note: Both the unit 1 and unit 2 assessment papers have 70 marks available so you have 1 minute 29 seconds for each mark. Therefore, you should spend approximately 15 minutes section C, a 12 mark essay. Make sure you leave enough time to do the essays.

Revision strategies

Do at least 5 past exam papers for each unit. Look at the mark schemes and examiners reports to see what the examiner wants.

Focus on what you find difficult to understand and get to grips with it.

Revise in 25 minutes chunks, with 5 minute breaks in the middle to keep your mind alert. Do not just read this revision guide. Active revision is more effective: Make notes, draw mind maps, record audio clips and write revision cards.

Remember to revise methodology i.e. research methods, types of design, levels of data, inferential tests and any practicals you carried out. You will be able to gain lots of marks for understanding scientific procedures and techniques.

Assessment objectives (taken from Edexcel specification)

AO1-Demonstrate a knowledge and understanding of scientific ideas, processes, techniques and procedures
AO2-Apply knowledge and understanding of scientific ideas, processes, techniques and procedures
AO3-Analyse, interpret and evaluate scientific information, idea and evidence

Evaluating Studies, Theories and Treatments

Studies

You can use GRAVE to help you evaluate a study.

Generalisability-How generalisable is the study? Are the participants in the sample representative of the wider population?

Reliability-How easy is the study to replicate and get similar results? If a study have a standardised procedure and was done under controlled conditions, then it is easy to replicate. A study is reliable if it has been replicated and similar results have been found.

Application to real life-Can the study explain real life events or be applied to real life situations.

Validity-Does the study have internal validity? Internal validity reflects on the experimenter's competence-The person who is doing the experiment's ability to carry out the study well. Was the experiment well-designed? Did any factors interfere with the experiment?

A study has **internal validity** when the material or procedures used in the research measured what they were supposed to measure. For example, in Milgram's experiment on obedience, participants had to giving increasing levels of electric shock to another person on the orders of an authority figure. The number of shocks the participants were prepared to give was a good indicator of their obedience level and so the study has construct validity (an indicator of internal validity).

Avoiding **demand characteristics** is important to ensure internal validity. Demand characteristics refer to when participants guess what a study is about and then change their behaviour. For example, a participant might guess that a study is on obedience and deliberately change their behaviour to show how easily people obey or to show how difficult it is to get people to obey.

A study has **experimental validity** if participants believe in the experimental situation. For example, in Milgram's study, if the participants believed they really were giving real electric shocks and thought that Mr. Wallace was another participant rather than a confederate, then the study has experimental validity (an indicator of internal validity).

If a study has predictive validity, then this is another indicator of internal validity. A study has **predictive validity** if it accurately predicts a result in the future. For example, if a person gains a high score on a test measuring racial prejudice and then engages in acts of discrimination, then the test has predictive validity.

Does the study have **external validity**? A study has external validity if the findings can be generalised to other situations and populations. If a study is done in participants' natural environment and involves a natural task that might be experienced in everyday life then it has **ecological validity**, which is an indicator of external validity.

Population validity relates to whether the sample can be generalised to the population it is meant to represent. For example, if you are looking at sixth form students' views on university tuition fees but only use a sample of private school students, then the sample lacks population validity. If a study has population validity then this is an indicator of external validity.

Ethics-Does the study have any ethical issues? Were participants protected from physical and psychological harm? Were participants given the right to withdraw? Did the participants give fully informed consent or were they deceived about any aspect of the study? Were the participants debriefed? Was the anonymity of the participants protected? Was the researcher competent to carry out the research?

You do not have to discuss all these points in your evaluation. For example, if there are no ethical issues then you don't need to discuss them. GRAVE is just a trigger to jog your memory and to help you evaluate.

You should also consider the objectivity and credibility of the research.

Objectivity- This refers to whether the study has collected data that is unbiased. Quantitative (numerical) data is likely to be impartial.

Credibility-This refers to whether the study is trustworthy. Research is more trustworthy if it is scientific, reliable, valid and unbiased.

Theories

You can use SEA to evaluate a theory.

Studies that support/contradict the theory. You can also make one evaluative point per study you use in your evaluation. Do not spend too long evaluating any studies as you have been asked to focus on evaluating the theory. Remember that a theory is someone's idea about how something works.

Explanation-What are the problems/limitations of the theory? Are there alternative explanations?

Application to real life-How can the study be applied to real life situations or events?

Treatments

You can use DESERT to help you evaluate a treatment.

Directive- Is the patient reliant on the therapist for all the answers? Is there a power imbalance? If the therapist has too much power then the treatment is directive.

Effectiveness-How effective is the therapy at treating the behaviour?

Side effects-Are there any side effects to the therapy?

Expense-How expensive is the therapy in terms of time and money?

Reasons-Does the therapy looks at the underlying causes/reasons for the behaviour?

Types of people-Does the therapy only work on certain types of people?

What level of detail should you give in an evaluation?

For a short-answer evaluation question, your answer should only contain evaluative points i.e. assume the examiner knows the material already.
However, when you have 8 or more marks for evaluating, then you are expected to give some description to set up your argument. For example, for an 8 mark question on evaluating a study, 4 marks are for describing those things that you are then going to evaluate i.e. if you are going to discuss generalisability, then you should talk about the sample and the population used. The other 4 marks are for evaluation.
For a 12 mark question, 6 marks are for showing knowledge and understanding and 6 marks are for evaluation.

Compare the following two answers:

Evaluate Milgram's basic study (4 marks)

Milgram used a volunteer sample, which is not representative of the wider population. The volunteers may have been more obedient than other participants as they had agreed to take part in the study and may have felt more obliged to continue (1 AO3 mark).
Milgram's study was reliable because it had a standardised procedure, which makes it easy to repeat and get the same results (1 AO3 mark).
The study has experimental validity, as the participants believed the shocks were real. The fact that participants showed signs of distress such as nervous showing that they believed the shocks were real (1 AO3 mark).
Milgram's study lacks ecological validity as it involved an artificial situation and mundane realism as people are not normally asked to give electric shocks to another person for wrong answers on a word pair task (1 AO3 mark).

Evaluate Milgram's basic study (8 marks)

Milgram was investigating obedience (1 AO1 mark). He recruited 40 male participants via an advert in a local newspaper (1 AO1 mark). This makes it difficult to generalise as it was an all-male, volunteer sample from the USA. The volunteers may have been more obedient than other participants as they had agreed to take part in the study and may have felt more obliged to continue. Furthermore, males are not representative of how females would behave (1 AO3 mark).
Participants were asked to give electric shocks to Mr. Wallace. They thought the shocks were real when they were fake and they believed that Mr. Wallace was another participant when he was in fact a confederate of the experimenter (1 AO1 mark). Therefore, the participants were deceived, which is an ethical issue (1 AO3 mark). The participants were given verbal prods to continue throughout the experiment (1 AO1 mark). Many experienced distress during the experiment but felt compelled to continue giving the electric shocks. Therefore, participants were not protected from psychological harm, which is another ethical issue (1 AO3 mark).
The experiment took place in a laboratory at Yale university and followed a standardised procedure (1 AO1 mark). The artificial situation means the study lacks ecological validity but the control over extraneous variables means the study has good internal validity (1 AO3 mark).

Note: AO1 marks are for knowledge and understanding and AO3 marks are for evaluating.

Chapter 1-Social Psychology

You need to be able to describe what the social psychology is about

Social psychology is about how our behaviour is affected by other people. At AS level, topics such as group behaviour, prejudice and obedience are covered. However, social psychology also covers topics such as why people help or do not help others, why people are attracted to certain people and crowd behaviour.

You need to be able to describe obedience

Obedience is when you follow orders given by a person with authority over you. Social psychologists have studied obedience to understand what makes people obey and the circumstances under which people are more obedient.

You need to be able to describe and evaluate Milgram's (1963) study of obedience

Description of basic study:

Aim-To investigate what level of obedience would be shown when participants were told by an authority figure to administer electric shocks to another person.

Procedure-A volunteer sample of 40 males aged between 20 and 50 years of age, were recruited from a newspaper advertisement. Participants were told that the study was about the effects of punishment on learning and that they would be paid $4.50 for taking part. When participants arrived at Yale University, they were asked to draw lots for who would have the role of teacher or learner in the experiment. The draw was set up so that the participant was always the teacher and Mr. Wallace (the confederate) was always the learner. Participants were then shown an electric shock generator, which had 30 switches from 15V to 450V. They were then asked to give increasing levels of electric shocks to the learner if he got any words incorrect on a word pair task. Unbeknown to the participants the electric shocks were fake. At certain voltages, Mr. Wallace pretended to show signs of pain. At 315V, Mr. Wallace became silent. Whenever the participants said they wanted to stop giving the electric shocks, they were given verbal prods to continue.

Results-100% (40/40) of the participants obeyed up to 300 volts and 65% (26/40) of the participants were fully obedient and gave all the shocks to 450V. During the study many participants showed distress at having to give the electric shocks.

Conclusion-People will obey authority figures even when it means causing harm to an innocent person. Milgram suggested the high levels of obedience in the study may have been due to the fact that the experiment took place at the prestigious Yale University. The participants may also have felt they should continue with the study because they had volunteered and were offered payment for their participation.

Evaluation:

Generalisability- All of Milgram's participants were volunteers who are likely to be more obedient than other participants so the sample is not generalisable in this respect.
It could also be argued that Milgram's study is not generalisable as it was only carried out on American males who are not representative of the wider population. However, when

Milgram tested females in exactly the same way, he found identical levels of obedience. Studies testing obedience across the world have found similar levels of obedience.

Reliability-Milgram's study was reliable because it had a standardised procedure, which makes it easy to repeat and get the same results. A script was followed and all participants heard the same recordings from Mr. Wallace. They were also give the same verbal prods such as 'You must continue' when they said they wanted to stop. This makes the study easily replicable.

Application to real life-The study can be applied to real life as it shows how under pressure people will obey an authority figure. The study has been used to explain why the Nazis were so obedient to Hitler even when it harmed innocent people. It can also explain why people are so obedient to their bosses at work even when it might cause harm to others such as firing colleagues.

Internal validity- The number of shocks participants were prepared to give was a good indicator of their obedience level and so the study has construct validity (an indicator of internal validity). The study has experimental validity, another indicator of internal validity, as the participants believed the shocks were real. The fact that participants showed signs of distress such as nervous laughter shows that their belief in the experimental situation was genuine. In fact, Milgram took great care to make sure his study had experimental validity so that the participants believed the situation was real. He rigged a draw with the participant and Mr. Wallace so that participants thought they had randomly been allocated the role of teacher. He also gave a sample 45V shock so that participants believed the shocks they were giving were real.

External validity-Some psychologists have suggested that Milgram's study lacks ecological validity as it involved an artificial situation. People do not usually attend a university to take part in a psychology experiment in everyday life. The study also lacks mundane realism as people are not normally asked to give electric shocks to another person for wrong answers on a word pair task. However, Milgram argued that the study does reflect how people behave in the real world as people do recognise authority figures and follow orders in the real world.

Ethics-One of the main criticisms of Milgram's study was the effects it had on participants. Participants did not give informed consent and were deceived. They were told that the aim of the study was to investigate the effects of punishment on learning when it was actually about obedience. They also thought they were giving real electric shocks when they were fake. Furthermore, participants were not protected from psychological harm as many experienced distress and may have felt bad about themselves after the experiment for being so obedient. They were also given verbal prods to continue throughout the experiment. However, Milgram did give participants the right to withdraw at the beginning of the experiment. He also thoroughly debriefed his participants and they were followed up a year later by psychiatrists. 84% of participants said they were glad or very glad to have taken part in the experiment.

Objectivity-Obedience was measured in terms of the level of shocks given on the shock generator. This is a quantitative and scientific way of measuring obedience and so the study is objective.

Credibility-The study was reliable, objective and scientific so it was credible in many ways. However, Milgram's study has been criticised for over-stating the obedience rate.

You need to be able to describe and evaluate the 'Telephonic instructions' (experiment 7) variation of Milgram's obedience studies

Description

Aim-To see if it is easier to resist the orders from an authority figure if they are not close by.

Procedure-The experimenter gave orders to participants over the telephone from another room. All other aspects of the study were the same.

Results-Obedience fell to 22.5% and many participants cheated and missed out shocks or gave less voltage than ordered to.

Conclusion-This shows that people are more obedient to authority figures who are close by.

Specific evaluative points for this variation: It can be applied to real life in that it shows that authority figures need to be present in order for levels of obedience to remain high. For example, students are more likely to be obedient if their teacher is close by.

You need to be able to describe and evaluate the 'Rundown office block' (Experiment 10) variation of Milgram's obedience studies

Description:

Aim-To see whether environment can influence levels of obedience.

Procedure-The experiment was conducted in an office suite in Bridgeport away from Yale university. Participants were told that a private research company was carrying out the study. All other aspects such as recruitment and payment were the same as in the original study.

Results-48% of the participants obeyed up to the maximum 450V.

Conclusion-Environment can influence levels of obedience.

Specific evaluative point for this variation: As this variation took place in the natural environment of an office block, it has higher ecological validity than the other variations, which took place in a laboratory.

You need to be able to describe and evaluate the 'Ordinary man give orders' (experiment 13) variation of Milgram's obedience studies

Description:

Aim-To see whether the status of the person giving orders affects obedience levels.

Procedure-This experiment involved two confederates. As in the original study, the draw was rigged so that Mr. Wallace received the fake electric shocks. The second confederate was then assigned the task of recording the time taken to give the shocks. A telephone call took the experimenter away from the laboratory and the experimenter told the participants to go on with the experiment until all the word pairs were learned perfectly (without mentioning which shock levels are to be used). The second confederate suggests a system for administering the shocks, specifically, to increase the shock level one step each time the learner makes a mistake.

Results-Only 20% of participants obeyed the ordinary man's orders.

Conclusion-People are less likely to obey orders from a person who is not perceived to be an authority figure.

Specific evaluative points for this variation: The study lacks credibility for the following reasons: The withdrawal of the experimenter from the laboratory was awkward. Even though the experimenter was absent, he had said to carry on with the experiment so the 'ordinary man' was only giving orders about the exact shock levels. He had not decided to administer the shocks himself.

Note: For the variations, you can make many of the same evaluative points as you would for the basic study.
For example, the study was reliable because it had a standardised procedure, which makes it easy to repeat and get the same results. A script was followed and all participants heard the same comments from Mr. Wallace. They were also give the same verbal prods such as 'You must continue' when they said they wanted to stop. This makes the study easily replicable.

Tip: Remember don't just say a study is reliable because it is easy to repeat and has a standardised procedure as you can say this about most laboratory experiments. Explain why this particular study is easy to repeat and give details.
Don't just say a study lacks ecological validity because it was done in an artificial environment. Explain what aspects of this particular study were artificial.

You need to be able to describe and evaluate agency theory as a theory of obedience

Description:

This theory says that we obey others in order to create a stable society. Milgram identifies two different states of being: The autonomous state, when our behaviour is controlled by our own free will and the agentic state, when we put aside our personal beliefs and wishes to obey authority figures. Milgram suggested that we acquire the agentic state in childhood as we become socialised at home and at school. The agentic shift refers to when people shift from an autonomous state when they are taking responsibility for their own actions to an agentic state when they pass this responsibility to the authority figure. If people believe the authority figure is legitimate such as a police officer or doctor, they are more likely to obey. They are also more likely to follow orders if they believe the authority figure will accept responsibility for what happens. Whilst in the agentic state we may experience moral strain. This is the sense that we are acting against our own beliefs. We might use a strategy called denial in order to cope.

Evaluation:

Studies-Milgram's study supports agency theory as it found that participants would obey an authority figure and give electric shocks to another person. Blass showed students an edited film of Milgram's study and questioned them about whether Milgram or his participants were more responsible for the shocks. Participants said Milgram was more responsible. This supports agency theory. Meeus and Raaijmaker's study found that participants would obey an authority figure and give negative remarks to someone they thought was a job applicant. This study supports the notion that people can be agents of authority and act against their own conscience.

Explanation-The idea that obedience helps to maintain as stable society makes sense. Agency theory explains a range of real-life situations in which people obey orders. However, Agency theory does not explain individual differences in obedience, for example why some people did not obey Milgram. 35% of participants did not give all the electric shocks. Furthermore, Agency theory does not explain why some people, who are not in a position of authority, can still be highly skilled in commanding obedience from other people. The theory of charismatic leadership is better at explaining why some people are particularly good at obtaining obedience from others. Some argue that agency theory is more a description of obedience rather than a detailed explanation. Social power offers another explanation of obedience. It explains how we are more likely to obey those with legitimate power over us or who have expert power. The concept of the agentic shift is hard to test experimentally, which reduces the credibility of the theory.

Application to real life-Agency theory can help to explain why the Nazis were so obedient to Hitler during the Holocaust. Eichmann said in his testimony that he was only following orders. It could also be used to explain why US soldiers tortured Iraqi prisoners in Abu Ghraib. Agency theory can also explain why people are willing to fire or reprimand their colleagues on the orders of their boss. The implications of agency theory are that training should be given to professionals such as nurses, police officers and the armed forces so that they don't obey authority figures without question.

You need to be able to describe and evaluate social impact theory as a theory of obedience

Description:

Social impact theory describes how people are influenced by others in social situations. The person or people doing the influencing are called the source(s) and the person or people being influenced are called the target(s). The greater the strength, immediacy and number of sources the greater the impact. The number of sources relates to the idea that the more people trying to influence you the greater their impact. For example, you may be persuaded to go to university if a large number of your friends and teachers argue that you should go. The strength of the sources relates to the status, expertise and power of the sources. For example, a message will be strengthened if the person doing the convincing is an expert in the field. A careers advisor who points out that it will increase your job prospects if you go to university is more likely to be listened to than a person with no expertise in the area. Immediacy relates to the physical and psychological distance of the source to the target. For example, a message will have more impact if it comes from friends rather than strangers due to their psychological immediacy. Your friend trying to convince you to go to university is going to have more impact than a person you've just met at a party. Social impact theory can be applied to obedience not just social influence.

For example, students might change their behaviour if the headmaster enters their classroom due to his status and physical immediacy to them.

The theory can be represented as a mathematical formula:

$i = f (SIN)$

Impact = function of (strength of the sources x immediacy of sources x number of sources)

Evaluation:

Studies-Sedikides and Jackson (1990) found that high strength sources (people with power and social status) and high immediacy sources (people who were psychologically or physically close) had more influence on the participants' opinions and behaviour than low-strength and low-immediacy sources. This supports social impact theory.
Milgram, Bickman, and Berkowitz (1969) investigated the influence of the number of confederates looking up at a building on the behaviour of people walking past. They found that more passers-by stopped as the size of the crowd looking up increased. This supports the idea that the more people persuading us to do something the more likely we will be influenced.

When Milgram moved his experiment from Yale university to a rundown office block in Bridgeport, obedience dropped as the experimenter/source's status or strength reduced. In the variation 'Ordinary man gives orders', in which the experimenter is called out of the room and asks an ordinary man to play his role and give orders. The number of teacher/targets shocking to the limit fell from 63% to 20% and so the intensity of impact fell as the strength of the source reduced. This supports Latane's theory that the strength of the source affects their impact.
In the variation, 'Telephonic Instructions', the experimenter gave orders over the telephone to administer the electric shocks. The immediacy of the experimenter was reduced and obedience dropped from 63% to 22.5%. This is in line with Latane's theory that the impact of the source is affected by their proximity (closeness) to the target.

Explanation-As the theory has a mathematical formula, it can be used to predict how obedient someone might be in a particular situation assuming we can measure the strength of the sources (e.g. their expertise or status), the immediacy of the sources (how close they are) and the number of sources. However, reducing obedience down to a mathematical formula may be too simplistic a way of understanding obedience as there are so many different factors that can affect it. The theory also ignores individual differences in obedience. Furthermore, it cannot predict what will happen if two equal groups impact on each other.

Application to real life-Social impact theory can explain a number of everyday situations where people are influenced by others. For example, we are more likely to be convinced that capital punishment is wrong if all of our friends are in agreement. Students are also more likely to obey a teacher if they are in the same room as them and if they have higher status in the school.

You need to be able to compare agency theory and social impact theory

Social impact theory explains the different factors involved in obedience better than agency theory. Social impact theory says that an individual's obedience is affected by the number of people trying to influence them, the sources' status, expertise and power and their immediacy to the individual in terms of physical and psychological distance. In contrast, agency theory is more a description of obedience than an explanation. It says that we obey authority figures when we are in the agentic state but it does not really explain how the agentic shift occurs.

Agency theory was designed to explain obedience whereas social impact theory is more a theory of social influence. Therefore, agency theory can better explain the different levels of obedience found in Milgram's variation studies as it is more focused on obedience.

Agency theory suggests that we have evolved to obey authority figures in order to maintain a stable society. Understanding obedience as an evolutionary mechanism helps us to understand why people may commit atrocities such as those during the Holocaust under the orders of an authority figure.

You need to be able to describe and evaluate one contemporary study. For example, Burger (2009) 'Would people still obey today?'

Description:

Aim-To replicate Milgram's finding and to see whether people would still obey today but under more ethical conditions.

Procedure-To ensure that all the participants were psychologically stable, Burger used a two-step screening process. Questionnaires filled out in step 1 were given to a clinical psychologist, who conducted an interview with the participants. Of the 123 people who participated in this second screening process, 47 (38.2%) were excluded from the study by the clinical psychologist.

In Burger's base condition, the experimental setup was the same as Milgram. There was a rigged draw to determine who would be the learner and who would be the teacher, with the confederate always made the learner. The confederate was strapped into a chair with electrodes attached. The teacher sat down in front of a shock machine asked to give increasing electric shocks to the learner when they got answers wrong on a word pair task. At 150V the confederate said 'Ugh. That's all. Get me out of here. I told you I had heart trouble. My heart's starting to bother me now. Get me out of here please. My heart's starting to bother me. I refuse to go on. Let me out.' The experimenter gave same prods as in Milgram's study, for example, 'The experiment requires that you continue' and, 'You have no other choice you must continue.' The experiment ended when either the teacher refused to continue or the teacher read the next item on the list of word pairs after having pressed the 150V switch. Burger argued that as the majority of participants in Milgram's study who went past 150V continued to 450V, then this was an indication of full obedience. Participants were then debriefed by being told the experiment was on obedience and that the electric shocks were fake. The confederate then entered the room to show the participants that he was fine.

Results-70% of participants had to be stopped after administering the 150V shock. It was predicted that they would have on to 450V.

Conclusion-People are just as likely to obey an authority figure and harm an innocent person today as when Milgram conducted his study. The same situational factors that led to obedience in Milgram's study affect obedience in the present day.

Evaluation:

Generalisability- All of Burger's participants were volunteers who are likely to be more obedient than other participants so the sample is not representative of the wider population. Furthermore, Burger's participants went through a double screening process to make sure they were psychologically stable. The participants who were allowed to take part may have been more obedient than average. However, Burger did use male and female participants from a very wide age range (20 to 81 years old), which make the sample more generalisable.

Reliability-Burger's study was reliable because it had a standardised procedure, which makes it easy to repeat and get the same results. A script was followed and all participants heard the same recordings from the confederate. They were also given the same verbal prods such as, 'The experiment requires that you continue,' when they said they wanted to stop. This makes the study easily replicable.

Application to real life-The study can be applied to real life as it shows how people under pressure will obey an authority figure. It can explain why people even in the present day are so obedient to authority figures. For example, people may obey their bosses at work to fire their colleagues even when it goes against their own wishes.

Internal validity- The number of shocks participants were prepared to give was a good indicator of their obedience level and so the study has construct validity (an indicator of internal validity). The study has experimental validity, another indicator of internal validity, as the participants believed the shocks were real. Like Milgram, Burger took care to make sure his study had experimental validity so that the participants believed the situation was real. He rigged a draw with the participant and confederate so that participants thought they had randomly been allocated the role of teacher. However, Burger gave his participants only a 15 volt sample shock instead of Milgram's 45 volts. This 'may have led them to assume that the shock generator was not really that shocking,' and may have made them more likely to obey.
External validity-Burger's study lacks ecological validity as it involved an artificial situation. People do not usually attend a university to take part in a psychology experiment in everyday life. The study also lacks mundane realism as people are not normally asked to give electric shocks to another person for wrong answers on a word pair task.

Ethics-Burger made great efforts to ensure his study was ethical. He stopped the study at 150 volts to ensure that the participants did not experience the intense stress that they did in the subsequent parts of Milgram's study. Burger also implemented a two-step screening processing to exclude anyone who might have a negative reaction to his study. Participants were told at least three times (twice in writing) that they could withdraw from the study at any time and still receive their $50 for participation. Participants were only given a mild 15 volt sample shock rather than the 45 volt shock in Milgram's study. As soon as the study ended, participants were informed that the learner had received no shocks and within a few seconds the learner entered the room to reassure the participant that he was fine. The experimenter who ran the study was also a clinical psychologist who knew he needed to stop the study if he saw signs of excessive stress.

Objectivity-Obedience was measured in terms of the level of shocks given on the shock generator. This is a quantitative and scientific way of measuring obedience and so the study is objective.

Credibility-The study was reliable, objective and scientific so it was credible in many ways. However, there is no certainty that participants who went to 150V would have continued to 450V as in Milgram's study.

You need to be able to describe individual differences in obedience and dissent/resistance to obedience

Individual differences in personality can affect obedience. Adorno (1950) suggested that an authoritarian personality type is more likely to obey an authority. These are people who tend to look up to those of higher status and look down on those of inferior status, they have more rigid opinions and beliefs and they are more suspicious and hostile. Milgram and Elms (1966) found that obedient participants were likely to have more authoritarian personalities (measured using the F-scale) than disobedient participants.
People who have an internal locus of control and believe that they are responsible for their own behaviour are less likely to obey. Dambrum & Vatine (2010) found that those who took more responsibility for their own behaviour rather than blaming others such as the experimenter, generally gave lower shocks in the Milgram experiment.
People with a higher level of education are also less likely to obey without question.
There does not appear to be any real difference between men and women in their ability to resist obeying an authority figure. Milgram (1963) found that men and women were equally obedient. Blass (1999) analysed the results of ten obedience studies using male and female participants and found that only one study reported a significant difference between men and women in levels of obedience. Kilham & Mann (1974) found that 40% of men and 16% of women were obedient in the Australian study.
Non-conformists are not aware of social norms or not bothered by them and so are less likely to feel the pressure to obey an authority figure. Anti-conformists, in contrast to non-conformists, deliberately go out of their way to not conform. This could be due to deeply held personal beliefs or perhaps just wanting to be seen as different. Anti-conformists are less likely to be obedient.

You need to be able to describe situational factors in obedience and dissent/resistance to obedience

Milgram demonstrated in his variation studies that situational factors have an effect on obedience. Milgram found that having a disobedient ally (a confederate) who refused to give the shocks led to only 10% of participants giving the full 450V. Running the experiment in a rundown office block rather than the prestigious Yale university or having an ordinary man give orders also reduced obedience. This suggests that the status of the authority figure affects obedience levels. The proximity of the authority figure was another factor in obedience. Participants were less likely to obey when the authority figure was not in the room.

You need to be able to describe cultural factors in obedience and dissent/resistance to obedience

Culture may have an impact on obedience. Individualistic cultures emphasize the importance of personal freedom and independence. Children are brought up to respect authority but they are also encouraged to be assertive. This can lead to lower levels of obedience in contrast to collectivist cultures, which place more emphasis on the wider group. In contrast, in collectivistic cultures, children are taught to conform to the majority and this is viewed positively as a way of connecting with others and becoming responsible for one's own actions. This suggests that people from collectivistic cultures should be more obedient. However, research into obedience in other cultures suggests that variations in obedience may be to do with how the studies were carried out rather than cultural differences. For example, Ancona and Paryeson (1968) found a higher obedience rate in Italy but they only used 330V as their maximum shock level.

You need to be able to describe what is meant by prejudice and discrimination

Prejudice: To form a judgement about a person before finding out anything about them as individuals. Prejudice is usually based on negative stereotypes about certain groups of people.

Discrimination: A behaviour towards another person based on prejudice.

You need to be able to describe and evaluate social identity theory

Description:

Social identity theory says that prejudice can arise from the mere existence of another group. Prejudice can be explained by our tendency to identify ourselves as part of a group and to classify other people as either within or outside that group. There are three stages to social identity theory: 1)Social Categorisation-This is when we categorise ourselves as being in a particular group often based on stereotypes. The group that we belong to is the in-group and any comparison group is the out-group. For example, when someone classifies themselves as a football supporter of a certain team, all other football teams are then viewed as the out-group.
2)Social Identification-This refers to when we identify with a particular group and adopt the behaviours of that group. We may also take on the group's values and norms. The way we view ourselves is affected by how well the group is doing relative to other groups. For example, a football supporter may adopting the behaviours of their club such as certain football chants and they may wear clothes that identify them as being part o the group such as wearing the club's scarf.
3)Social Comparison-Comparing our own group (the in-group) more favourably against other groups (out-groups) to boost our self-esteem. For example, football supporters viewing their team as the best. This can lead to discrimination and sometimes even dehumanisation of the out-group. Football supporters of one football team may even end up fighting supporters of a different football team.

Evaluation:

Studies- Tajfel et al.'s (1971) minimal groups study found that boys overwhelmingly chose to allocate points to boys who had been identified as in the same group as themselves, which supports social identity theory. Poppe and Linssen found that Eastern Europeans favour their own country over other Eastern Europeans, which supports the idea that people show in-group favouritism. Sherifs' Robbers Cave study provides further evidence for social identity theory in that the two groups of boys showed prejudice to the boys not in their group even before competition was introduced. Crocker and Luhtanen's (1990) study also supports social identity theory as it found that people tend to have high self-esteem if they think well of the group to which they belong. On the other hand, Dobbs and Crano's (2001) study contradicts social identity theory as it found that mere categorisation of people into groups is not always sufficient to create in group favouritism.

Explanation- However, social identity theory does not explain individual differences in prejudice. Some people are much more prejudiced than others to people in the out-group. Realistic conflict theory may be a better explanation of prejudice. It says that people become prejudiced when there is 'competition over scarce resources'. This may explain prejudice in competitive situations better.

Application to real life- Social identity theory has face validity as it can explain behaviour real life prejudice such as racism, snobbery and football violence.

You need to be able to describe and evaluate realistic conflict theory as a theory of prejudice

Description:

Realistic conflict theory says that prejudice occurs between different groups of people when there is competition over limited resources. So if two groups want the same thing but only one group can have it, conflict can arise. The group to which you belong is called the in-group. The others are thought of as the out-group. People tend to favour members of their own in-group and be hostile towards the out-group. People may also over-estimate their in-group's achievements and abilities. Prejudice can be reduced when groups have to work together to solve a problem. A superordinate goal is a something that can only be achieved by the groups working together cooperatively. Superordinate goals help to reduce prejudice.

Evaluation:

Studies- Sherif's Robber's Cave study supports realistic conflict theory as the boys became particularly hostile to each other during the tournament.
Explanation- The theory has face validity as groups do seem to become hostile towards each other in real life when there is competition over a scarce resource e.g. land, a football cup.
Realistic conflict theory can better explain widespread prejudice compared to the authoritarian personality approach. The boys in the Robber's Cave study could not all have had authoritarian personalities but they all became prejudiced to the out-group.

Application to real life-Realistic conflict theory can explain why groups in competition with each other can become very hostile towards each other such as the supporters of rival football teams.

You need to be able to describe and evaluate the classic study by Sherif (1954/1961) 'Intergroup conflict and cooperation: The Robbers Cave Experiment'

Aim-To see whether it is possible to create prejudice between two similar groups when they are put in competition with each other and to see if prejudice can be reduced through getting the groups to work together to achieve a superordinate goal (a goal that can only be achieved through cooperative working).

Procedure-Twenty-two eleven year-old boys were chosen to take part because they were well-adjusted. They were all from a similar background. Before the start of the experiment, the boys were randomly divided into two groups with eleven boys each.
The two groups of boys were taken to a summer camp in Robbers Cave State Park in Oklahoma. Initially, each group did not know the existence of the other group. In the first

week the groups spent time bonding with each other while hiking in the park or swimming. Each group was asked to decide on a group name. One group chose the name Eagles and the other group chose the name Rattlers. The names were stencilled on to their flags and shirts to help build a sense of in-group identity.

During the second phase of the experiment, the two groups found out about each other's existence. A tournament with prizes was set up to create in-group favouritism. There was so much conflict between the two groups, phase two was cut short.

In phase three, the experimenters attempted to bring about cooperation between the two groups by getting them to work towards superordinate goals (task that can only be achieved by working together). The two groups were told that they had to work together to restore the drinking water supply as it had been damaged by vandals.

Results-The boys developed a strong in-group preference and even before the tournament started, the groups were fighting each other and calling each other names. The competition increased the antagonism between the two groups. The group that lost the tournament even stole the prizes of the winning group.

After the groups had to cooperate with the each other in phase three, tension between the groups diminished.

Conclusion-Competition increased prejudice and led to conflict between the two groups. Cooperation reduced conflict between the two groups.

Evaluation:

Generalisability-The study lacks generalisability as it only consisted of young boys who are not representative of the wider population. If the study was done with girls they may not have acted the same, as girls are often thought to be less competitive than boys.

Reliability-The study would be hard to replicate as it was a field study. Extraneous variables in the natural environment of the summer camp could have affected results. For example, if there was storm during the tournament that might have affected the boy's behaviour. However, Sherif et al. some elements of the study are easy to replicate, for example, they carefully controlled how long the boys had to bond and when they introduced the competition element of the study.

Application to real life-The study can be applied to real life by helping reduce prejudice between groups in society through use of superordinate goals.

Validity-This field study has high ecological validity as the boys were in a natural setting of a summer camp. The study also has experimental validity as the boys were unaware they were being observed and so would not have shown demand characteristics.

Note: Demand characteristics occur when participants guess the aim of the study and change their behaviour to please the researchers.

Ethics-There are ethical issues with Sherif's study. The researcher's deliberately created prejudice between the two groups of boys and this led to name-calling and even fighting between the boys. Therefore, the boys were not protected from psychological and physical harm. The boys did not know they were in the study and were not offered the right to withdraw. Although parents gave consent for the study, they did not know the full details of the study and probably would not have been happy at the idea of their boys being placed in situation where conflict was likely to occur.

You need to be able to describe one key question in social psychology. For example, 'How can social psychology be used to explain heroism?'

Zimbardo defines heroism as having four key elements: It is performed to help others in need; it is done voluntarily; it is performed even when the person knows they are at risk of psychological or physical harm and it is done without expectation of a reward. Understanding heroism and encouraging people to be heroic can have a positive impact on society.

Zimbardo founded the Heroic Imagination Project to research heroism and to learn how to train people to develop the characteristics of heroes. He also wanted to understand how to prevent the negative aspects of social influence such as the bystander effect, where people don't take responsibility for helping someone in need. His research has shown that 20% of people qualify as heroes. The most common acts of heroism are helping another person in an emergency and whistle-blowing on an injustice. Research has also found that volunteers, more educated people and those who have survived a disaster or trauma are more likely to be heroes. There are also factors that might stop us helping others such feeling powerless to change the world around us, anxiety about being rejected by other people for speaking out and relying on other people to take responsibility in difficult situations.

Linking the key questions to theories, concepts and studies:

Milgram's study shows how obedient people are to authority figures. As a result, they may feel unable to speak out against a destructive authority figure.

Sherif's study shows how we tend to favour our own in-group, which can prevent us helping those outside our group.

Social impact theory suggests that we are more likely to obey if the authority figures are nearby, great in number and legitimate. It may be hard to speak out against destructive authority in such situations.

The bystander effect refers to when people choose not to help someone in need because they rely on other people to take responsibility. Latane and Darley (1970) found that people are less likely to help a person in trouble if there are other people around. They said this was due to a 'diffusion of responsibility'.

Note: You may have to apply concepts, theories and/or research to a completely new issue/scenario in the exam that you have not studied.

You need to able to describe a practical you conducted in social psychology: A questionnaire collecting both quantitative data and qualitative data on in-group/out-group attitudes based age

Aim: To investigate in-group behaviour and whether participants show an in-group bias towards those of the same age as them.

Alternative directional hypothesis: Participants will have more positive attitudes towards people of the same age as them. People in a young age group (25 and under) will have more positive attitudes towards people in their own age group compared to people in an older age group (60+)

Null hypothesis: There will be no significant difference in the participants' attitudes towards people in a different age group to them. Participants who are 25 and under will not show an in-group preference for their own age group compared to the older age group (60+).

Sampling: An opportunity sample was used drawing on students from the sixth form. The sample size was 20 and they were all students between 16-17 years old. 9 males and 11 females were used.

Ethics: The participants were briefed before the questionnaire was administered and fully informed consent was obtained. They were given the right to withdraw during and after the questionnaire. They were also debriefed at the end of the questionnaire. Participants were assured that their responses would be kept anonymous and confidential as they were answering questions about their personal beliefs and attitudes.

Procedure: A questionnaire was designed to test participants' in-group attitudes towards people of the same age as them and out-group attitudes towards people of a different age to them. The questionnaire used a Likert scale to collect quantitative data about participants in-group/out-group attitudes and it also had four open questions to collect qualitative data. A pilot study was undertaken on three people to make sure the questions on the questionnaire were clear and unambiguous and to establish the reliability and validity of the questionnaire. 20 participants completed the questionnaire with the researcher present in small groups. Participants were briefed before the questionnaire and they completed it in silence so that they could not discuss answers. Participants were given the right to withdraw and debriefed at the end of the questionnaire. The quantitative part of the questionnaire was scored to measure attitudes to the in-group and attitudes to the out-group. The qualitative responses were analysed to look for dominant themes.

Results:

Quantitative research:

Attitude Score	Positive attitude to in-group	Positive attitude to out-group
Mean	3.4	2.4
Median	3.2	2.2
Mode	3.8	2.6
Range	1.4	1.2

Participants had a more positive attitude towards people of the same age as them. The mean score for positive attitude to the in-group was 3.4 compared to 2.4 for the out-group.

Qualitative research:

One theme was that younger people dress better.

Another theme was that younger people are more adaptable to change. For example, younger people are better with new technology.

Conclusion: The results suggest that younger people do favour those of the same age as them and have more negative attitudes towards people of a different age to them. Social identity theory suggests we prefer our in-group and devalue the out-group. Ageism is an example of this in-group preference.

Evaluation:

Participants may have given socially desirable answers on the questionnaire so that they did not appear too prejudiced to the out-group even though they might have been privately. Participants may have been influenced by the age of the researcher carrying out the questionnaire. There can be problems with the Likert scale in collecting data on attitudes as participants can be inclined to give answers towards the middle of the scale rather than at the extremes, which could have affected overall scores. As an opportunity sample was used the sample may be unrepresentative of the wider population. There may also have been subjective interpretation of the qualitative data. Personal views and experience may have affected how the qualitative data was interpreted leading to a biased report being made.

You need to be able to describe and evaluate surveys

Surveys are used to find out about people's opinions and attitudes. Questionnaires and interviews are types of surveys and are used to gather self-report data.

Questionnaires

Description:

Questionnaires involve written questions to find out about people's views and opinions. They are able to collect data from lots of people as everyone is asked the same questions and can answer them in their own time. Questionnaires can be sent by post, filled in on the internet, given face-to-face or left in a public place for people to pick up. The questions can either be closed or open. Closed questions may involve a Likert type scale or yes/no questions. Open questions ask people to explain what they think about a certain topic in their own words. If closed questions are used then quantitative data can be obtained. If open questions are used then qualitative data can be obtained.

Evaluation:

Questionnaires allow data to be gathered from large samples without too much cost. If closed questions are used, the quantitative data can be statistically analysed. It is also easy to compare the data from closed questionnaires as everyone answers the same questions. Furthermore, questionnaires with closed questions can be easy to replicate. A test-retest method can be used to establish the external reliability of a questionnaire. This is when the same people are given a questionnaire on different days to see if they give the same responses. If they give the same responses this shows that the questionnaire has external reliability.

Questionnaires with open questions can collect rich, qualitative data but they are harder to replicate. People are unlikely to give exactly the same responses to questions such as 'What do you think about your school?' on different days. Therefore, questionnaires with open questions tend to have less external reliability.

If a questionnaire has internal reliability then all the questions should be measuring the same concept. For example, if a questionnaire is looking at empathy, then all the questions should relate to this personality characteristic. The internal reliability of a questionnaire can be assessed using a split-half method. This involves splitting the questionnaire up into two halves and seeing whether participants' scores on both halves of the questionnaire are the same. If the participants have a similar score for empathy on both halves of the questionnaire, then it has internal reliability.

A key problem with questionnaires is that people may give socially desirable answers because they want the researchers to think well of them. Participants may also misunderstand the questions and interpret the questions differently. Questions asked beforehand could affect later answers. Questionnaires with closed questions can limit participants' responses, which affects validity. Questionnaires with open questions are open to interpretation.

Sometimes the questions may not be measuring what they were intended to measure. A questionnaire has face validity if the questions make sense in terms of what they are trying to measure. For example, if a questionnaire is looking at aggression and participants are asked how often they swear as a measure of aggression, the questionnaire may lack validity. This is because some people may swear as a means of expression rather than out of aggression. A questionnaire has predictive validity if it can predict future behaviour. For example, a questionnaire looking at helpfulness should be able to predict future helping behaviour. A questionnaire has concurrent validity if a different questionnaire is used and it finds similar results. For example, if two different questionnaires are used to measure competitiveness and they both suggest that the person is competitive then they have concurrent validity.

Unstructured, structured and semi-structured interviews

Description:

An interview involves asking participants questions verbally face-to face.

Structured interviews involve closed questions and produce quantitative data. Questions are decided upon in advance and all participant answer the questions in the same order. Unstructured interviews involve open questions and produce qualitative data. A couple of questions are decided on in advance but the researcher adapts their questions based on participants' responses. An unstructured interview often involves an in-depth discussion on a certain topic. Semi-structured interviews have prepared questions but allow participants to expand on some of their answers.

Evaluation:

Structured interviews allow quantitative data to be obtained, which can be statistically analysed. Unlike questionnaires, interviews allow the researcher to explain any questions that have been misunderstood. Unstructured interviews allow rich, detailed information to be obtained about people's opinions and views. Participants can expand on their answers and the researcher can follow up on any issues raised.

A disadvantage of interviews is that participants may give socially desirable answers to appear in a good light. Structured interviews can also limit participants' responses. Unstructured interviews are open to interpretation and bias. Furthermore, interviews can be time-consuming and expensive as they need to be delivered face-to-face.

You need to be able to describe and evaluate quantitative and qualitative data

Studies that focus on producing numerical results or data that can in some way be 'counted' (quantified) are described as quantitative research. Such studies tend to use large samples of people or animals so that results can be generalised to the wider population. Experiments, questionnaires and structured interviews are good sources of quantitative data. Quantitative data are measurable and firm conclusions can be drawn from the data. Statistical tests can be done to see how far the results are likely to be due to chance. In experiments, the independent variable is manipulated and the dependent variable is measured. Variables are also carefully operationalised and there are good controls. This makes the research more scientific. If a quantitative research is repeated, often the same data will be found. This shows that quantitative data is reliable. However, the careful operationalising of variables in quantitative research means that real life events and interactions are not being measured (lack of validity).
In comparison, qualitative data can be gathered in more natural situations and reflects real life behaviour more. So where quantitative data can have a lack of validity, qualitative data can be more valid. Qualitative data can be gathered from case studies, unstructured interviews and observations in participants' natural environments. However, qualitative data is harder to replicate and can lack reliability.

You need to be able to explain how different research methods produce qualitative and quantitative data

Structured interviews and questionnaires give quantitative data because they involve set closed questions. The questions have yes/no answers or are rated on a scale such as the Likert scale (where participants can give answers from strongly agree to strongly disagree and these answers can be scored). This gives numerical data, which is quantitative. Unstructured interviews and questionnaires use open questions and are good sources of qualitative data. For example, unstructured interviews may begin with a particular topic but then proceed like a conversation. They do not have set questions. The interviewer can explore areas that come up. No numerical data is obtained so the data is qualitative. An unstructured questionnaire would have open questions and then researchers would look for themes emerging from the participants' answers.

You need to be able to calculate measures of central tendency: mean, median and mode

The mean

The mean is often referred to as the average of a set of numbers. You calculate the mean by adding up all the numbers and then dividing by the number of numbers.

Consider the following data set: 12, 17, 23, 27

Add the numbers together: 12+17+23+27=79
Divide 79 by 4: 79/4 =19.75

The 'Mean' (Average) is 19.75

The median

The median is the 'middle value' in a list of numbers. To find the median, your numbers have to be listed in numerical order. If you have an odd number of numbers, the median is the middle entry in the list. If you have an even number of numbers, the median is equal to the sum of the two middle numbers divided by two.

Consider the following data set: 13, 17, 21, 8

Sort the numbers into numerical order: 8, 13, 17, 21

There is not a single middle number in this data set as there is an even number of numbers. Therefore, add the two middle numbers, 13 and 17, and divide by two:

13+17=30
30/2=15

The median is 15

The mode

The mode is the number that occurs most frequently in a set of data. If no number is repeated, then there is no mode for the set of data.

You need to be able to calculate measures of dispersion: range and standard deviation

The range

Note: The range is a measure of dispersion. It refers to how the data is spread out or 'dispersed'.

The range is the difference between the largest and smallest numbers.

Consider the following data set: 11, 15, 16, 21

Subtract the smallest number from the largest number: 21-11=10

The range is 10

Standard deviation

The standard deviation is a way of telling how far apart or how close together the data is.

Why are we interested in standard deviation?

Consider the following two data sets:
Data set 1: 28, 29, 30, 31, 32   Mean = (28+29+30+31+32)/5=30
Data set 2: 10, 20, 30, 40, 50   Mean = (10+20+30+40+50)/5=30

Both data sets have a mean of 30 but the data is spread much further apart in data set 2. Therefore, data set 2 has a larger standard deviation.

Standard deviation is a measure of dispersion, which means it's useful in determining how spread out the data is. For example, if one school has students who end up with a high mean number of UCAS points and a very small standard deviation, that means that the all the students at this school got good A-levels. If a second school has students that have an equally high mean number of UCAS points with a very high standard deviation as well, that means that the students had a much wider range of A-level grades with some getting high grades and some getting much worse grades. UCAS points with a very high standard deviation as well, that means that the students had a much wider range of A-level grades with some getting high grades and some getting much worse grades.

Calculating standard deviation

$$s = \sqrt{\frac{\sum(x - \bar{x})^2}{n - 1}}$$

X= each value
$\bar{X}$= mean of the data set
n = the number of values
$\sum$=sum of
For example, for the data set 46, 42, 44, 45 ,43:
1) Calculate the mean: $\bar{X}$ = (46+42+44+45+43)/5=44
2) Take away the mean from each value (x - $\bar{X}$) and then square it.
3) Add up all the (x - $\bar{X}$)^2 values 4+4+0+1+1=10
4) Divide the sum of all the (x - $\bar{X}$)^2 values by n-1: 10/(5-1)=10/4=2.5
5) Square root it all for the standard deviation, s. $\sqrt{}$ 2.5= 1.6

Note: Using a table can help you get your calculation right.

X	$\bar{X}$	(X - $\bar{X}$)	(X - $\bar{X}$)2
46	44	2	4
42	44	-2	4
44	44	0	0
45	44	1	1
43	44	-1	1

$\bar{X}$ = 44 $\sum$ = 10

$$s = \sqrt{\frac{\sum(X - \bar{X})^2}{n - 1}} = 1.6$$

How can you interpret standard deviation?

For datasets that have a normal distribution the standard deviation can be used to determine the proportion of values that lie within a particular range of the mean value. For such distributions, 68% of values are less than one standard deviation (1SD) away from the mean value, 95% of values are less than two standard deviations (2SD) away from the mean and 99% of values are less than three standard deviations (3SD) away from the mean.

The mean of our data set was 44 and the standard deviation (SD) is 1.6. Therefore, 68% of values in the data set lie between mean-1SD (44-1.6 =42.4) and mean +1SD (44+1.6=45.6). 99% of the values will lie between mean-3SD (44-4.8=39.2) and mean +3SD (44+4.8=48.8).

If the data set had the same mean of 44 but a larger standard deviation e.g. 2.4, it would suggest that the values were more dispersed.

You need to be able to understand normal distributions and skewed distributions

Data can be spread out in different ways. For example, it can be spread to the left or spread to the right. Normal distributions have data, which is symmetric around the mean and the mean, median and mode are equal. IQ follows a normal distribution. Most people have an IQ between 70 and 130 with a mean, median and mode of 100. Only a small percentage of people have an IQ under 70 or over 130.

If a distribution is skewed, then the mean is usually not in the middle.

For example, ten participants take part in a memory test and are asked to remember a list of 20 words. The mean of their scores was 9 but the median was 12. A distribution that is skewed to the left has mean that is smaller than the median i.e. it has a 'tail' on the left hand side.

A distribution that is skewed to the right has a mean that is larger than the median. This is common for a distribution that is skewed to the right i.e. it has a 'tail' stretching on the right hand side.

You need to be able to analyse qualitative data using thematic analysis

Qualitative data can be analysed using thematic analysis. A thematic analysis involves looking for 'themes' in descriptive text. For example, if an interview has been carried out, a researcher would look for themes in the interview transcript. The researcher would then identify, analyse and report patterns within the data.

An inductive thematic analysis would involve the researcher reading and re-reading the transcript until certain themes emerged.

In contrast, in a deductive thematic analysis, the researcher would decide what themes they were going to look for before they started analysing the transcript.

There are a number of stages in carrying out a thematic analysis: 1) The researcher familiarises themself with the data by reading it several times; 2) Initial codes are generated based on prominent features of the data; 3) The researcher looks for themes by examining the codes and collated data to identify broader patterns of meaning (potential themes); 4) The themes are reviewed by checking them against what people have said. At this stage, themes may be refined or discarded; 5) Themes are named and a detailed analysis of each theme is carried out; 6) Finally, the themes are written up with quotes from the data collected. The analysis is linked to existing theories.

Evaluation:

A thematic analysis can be used for a wide range of research questions. Rich, detailed data can be obtained, which can lead to a deeper insight into people's experiences, opinions and representations. However, thematic analyses are open to interpretation and hence subjective. They can be hard to replicate and so they have problems with reliability.

You need to be able to describe and evaluate sampling techniques

Description:

Random Sample-Each member of the population has an equal chance of being selected. For a small sample, you might draw names out of a hat/container. For a large sample, you might use birth records or the electoral role, allocate everyone a number and then get a random number generator to select certain people.

Self-Selected Sampling-You advertise for participants with specific characteristics e.g women over forty and they participants self-select themselves if they have those characteristics to take part in the study.

Opportunity Sample-This is when you select people based on who is available at a given time, often friends and family.

Stratified Sample-To ensure a cross-section of the target population is picked. For example, if you wanted to investigate the general population's attitude to childcare, you would select the right number of young females, young males, older males etc. that represents the proportion of them in the general population. Other criteria might include geographical locations and racial origins.

Volunteer Sample-This is when your sample consists of a group of participants who have chosen to take part.

Evaluation:

Random sample-Everyone in the chosen population has a chance of being in the sample. This is the best way of getting fair representation. However, if not everyone is in the sample, so there is still a chance that it will be biased (e.g. regarding age).

Systematic Sample-This is a manageable way of sampling. For example, if you choose every fifth person who comes along, this is a practical solution and reasonably fair as you will not be biased by personal preferences. This often involves people in one situation at a particular time e.g. walking down the High Street on Saturday morning, and this can cause bias.

Opportunity Sample-It is manageable and quick, as you can choose whoever is available. This often means friends and acquaintances. However, family and friends might be too cooperative and this might give bias to the findings as the participants are more likely to say what they think is wanted.

Stratified Sample-The required types of people are selected and there will be a spread of different types (using the desired criteria), whereas other types of sampling may not ensure this. However, choosing certain criteria and then finding people that fit those criteria does not necessarily mean that the people selected are representative of those criteria-they may have individual differences that give bias.

Volunteer Sample and Self-Selected Sample-This can be more ethical as the participants are interested in the study and can feel they are part of what is happening. However, volunteers are likely to be particular types of people, if only because they have time to take part in the study. They are not likely to be representative of the whole population.

You need to be able to describe the British Psychology Society code of ethics and conduct (2009) including risk management when carrying out research in psychology

Informed consent: Participants should be told about what the procedure entails and the aims of the study.

Debriefing: At the end of a study, participants should be told about any aspects of the study they were not informed about at the start. Participants should also be told about expected results and given the right to withdraw their data. The researchers should also check that the participants have not experienced any psychological harm.

Right to withdraw: Participants must be given the right to withdraw from the study at any time and given the option to withdraw their data at the end.

Deception: Participants should not be deceived about the aims of the study, what the procedure entails, the role of other participants or how their results will be used. Sometimes, it may be necessary to deceive participants about the aim of the study in order to investigate certain topics such as obedience. However, participants should only be deceived if they are not likely to come to any harm.

Protection from harm: Participants should be protected from physical and psychological harm. Psychological harm included distress and damage to self-image. The risk of harm should be no more than participants might expect in everyday life.

Confidentiality: All data should be confidential and anonymous. When data is collected, participants' names should not be recorded and numbers or pseudonyms used instead to ensure anonymity.

Competence: Researchers should be qualified and have the experience necessary to carry out the research.

Risk management: Researchers need to consider whether the study they wish to conduct exposes the participants to any greater risk than they would be exposed to in their normal lifestyle. They should also think about whether the research could cause the participants distress or self-doubt. A risk assessment should be carried out before conducting any research and the researcher should show an awareness of the power imbalance between themselves and their participants.

Exemplar exam questions:

Apply concepts, theories and research in the social approach to the problem of terrorism. (6 marks)

Student answer:

Terrorists may believe they are the in-group based on religion, race or political beliefs. Other people are in the out-group.

Social identity theory can be used to explain terrorism. Terrorists may categorise themselves as belonging to an in group based on religion, race or political beliefs and categorise people of other religions, race or political beliefs as being the out-group. They identify strongly with their in-group by taking on their values, beliefs and appearance. The terrorists may the compare themselves more favourably the out-group in order to boost their self-esteem. Terrorists may focus on the fact people from other religions are more immoral or greedy and this feeling of superiority might lead them to dehumanise the out-group so much that they are willing to kill them in an act of terrorism.

Realistic conflict theory explains how competition over resources can lead to conflict between groups. This theory explains terrorism as being related to competition over resources such as land. For example, the IRA wanted Northern Ireland to be governed by an Irish government not a British government. The IRA became so hostile towards the British government that they classed all British citizens as the out-group and bombed certain places in England.

Sherif's study showed how prejudice can occur between rival groups. Two groups of boys at a summer camp were put in competition with each other and prejudice quickly led to fighting and name-calling. This relates to how groups in competition with each other might commit terrorist acts against each other.

5/6 marks

Commentary:

This student applies their knowledge of social identity theory, realistic conflict theory and the Sherif study to terrorism well. One extra mark could have been gained by referring to agency theory. Agency theory might explain terrorism in terms of obedience to authority figures. People may commit acts of terrorism on the orders of their leader who they view as an authority figure. They may feel moral strain at committing the acts of terrorism.

Explain one key question for society in terms of concepts, theories or studies from the social approach (6 marks)

Student answer:

One key question is whether social psychology can be used to explain heroism. This is an important question as understanding heroism and encouraging people to be heroic can have a positive impact on society. One study that helps us understand why it is difficult to be a hero is Milgram's (1963) study on obedience. Milgram found that people would obey an authority figure even when they believed they were causing harm to an innocent person. Such studies can be used to teach people when it is important to disobey. Whistleblowers who are willing to speak out against corruption in public services or in companies are society's heroes because they go against authority. Agency theory says that we are socialised to obey from childhood as this helps to create a stable society. In the agentic state, we put aside our personal beliefs and wishes to obey authority figures. If people believe the authority figure is legitimate such as a police officer or doctor, they are more likely to obey. They are also more likely to follow orders if they believe the authority figure will accept responsibility for what happens. Encouraging people to take responsibility for their own actions can help people to behave like heroes. The bystander effect refers to when people choose not to help someone in need because they rely on other people to take responsibility. Latane and Darley (1970) found that people are less likely to help a person in trouble if there are other people around. When people stop expecting others to take responsibility, then they are more likely to help people in need. Social identity theory says that we favour our own in-group over comparable out-groups. This means that we are less likely to help those who we perceive to be in a different group to us. Overcoming these negative influences on our behaviour can enable us to act heroically towards those who we perceive to be different.

6/6 marks

Commentary:

This student applies both studies and theories to the key question. They also justify why these concepts relate to the key question in their answer, which is important as the exam question requires the student to 'explain'. There are other studies and theories that could have been referred to but there is enough here for 6 marks.

Chapter 2-Cognitive Psychology

You need to be able to describe what the cognitive approach is about

The cognitive approach studies how we process information. One of the assumptions of the cognitive approach is that the human mind can be seen as a system for handling information. Information from the environment is interpreted to make sense of it. Thinking, perceiving, using language and memorising are all ways of processing information.

Information processing occurs when information is taken in by the senses (input) and processed by the brain. Once the brain has processed the information, there is an output in some form.

Psychologists use a computer metaphor to describe how the brain processes information. Like a computer, the mind has an input in the form of senses, a store in the form of memory and an output in the form of behaviour. Cognitive processes are like computer software.

You need to be able to describe and evaluate the working memory model (Baddeley and Hitch, 1974)

Description:

The working memory model (Baddeley and Hitch, 1974) suggests that we have an active memory store that holds and manipulate information that is currently being thought about. The term 'working memory' reflects the concept that stored information is being worked on. The original model consisted of three separate components: the central executive, phonological loop and visuo-spatial sketchpad. The central executive is responsible for the control and coordination of mental operations including reasoning, comprehension, learning and memory. It can process information in different forms, for example, by sound, touch, sight etc. so it is modality free. It has a limited capacity, which means that it can only attend to a certain number of things at a time. Originally, the central executive was seen as only monitoring and coordinating the phonological loop and visuo-spatial sketch pad (slave stores) it is now believed to control our attention, allowing us to switch our attention from one thing to another.

The phonological loop deals with verbal material. It consists of two parts: a phonological store (inner ear), which is used to store speech-based sounds for a few seconds and an articulatory rehearsal system (inner voice), which is used to rehearse verbal information in our heads rather than out loud.

The visuo-spatial sketchpad (inner eye) stores and processes visual and spatial information.

The phonological loop and visuo-spatial sketchpad process information independently. Therefore, processing visual information should not interfere with processing verbal information.

Note: The phonological similarity effect refers to difficulty with remembering words that sound similar. This supports the view that the phonological store processes information by sound (acoustically).

The word length effect refers to being able to remember short monosyllabic words better than longer polysyllabic words. This supports the view that the articulatory rehearsal system has limited capacity.

People with a specific language impairment (SLI) have problems dealing with language. They do worse on language-based tasks than their IQ would suggest. Research has shown that children with SLI find it difficult to learn non-words such as blit because they have a deficit in their phonological loop, which stops them being able to learn and understand new words.

Evaluation:

Studies-Baddeley and Hitch carried out a number of experiments to see whether people could perform an irrelevant short-term memory task at the same time as cognitive task that involved learning new information, reasoning or understanding language. These experiments were called dual task experiments because they required participants to perform two tasks at the the same time. For example, in one experiment participants had to remember a sequence of random numbers while completing a verbal reasoning task. They found that participants found it difficult to carry out the verbal reasoning task when the number sequences were longer. From this, Baddeley and Hitch concluded that we have a limited capacity working memory system, which is able to both carry out mental operations and hold information temporarily. Baddeley and Hitch also found that when participants were asked to perform tasks that involved different types of processing, for example verbal and visual, their ability to carry out the tasks was not affected. This supports the idea that we have different visual and verbal systems within working memory for different types of task.

Case studies of brain-damaged patients (neurophysiological evidence) have been used to support the idea that working memory consists of different sub-systems. After a motorbike accident, KF had a digit span of one, suggesting that his phonological store was damaged. However, his visual memory was fine. In contrast, after a brain operation that was supposed to help his epilepsy, HM had problems with his visual memory but not verbal memory. These case studies provide evidence for separate visual and verbal systems within working memory.

Brain scans (neuroimaging) have also been used to support the idea of different sub-components within working memory. Paulesu et al. (1993) used PET scans to measure blood flow in different regions of the brain. He found that different parts of the brain are activated when participants are asked to carry out verbal (phonological) and non-verbal memory tasks. He identified the Broca's area and the supramarginal gyrus areas of the brain as being involved in phonological memory tasks. He then wanted to see whether he could identify which areas of the brain are used by the articulatory rehearsal system and the phonological store (sub-components of the phonological loop). In order to find this out, he asked participants to carry out a rhyme judgement task involving the articulatory rehearsal loop but not the phonological store. The Broca's area of the brain was activated when participants carried out the task. He concluded that the Broca's area can be identified with the articulatory rehearsal system. By using a subtraction method, he deduced that the supramarginal gyrus is related to the phonological store.

Explanation-A problem with the original model of working memory is that it could not explain how the working memory system could keep track of all the information across the different sub-systems and sub-components. In order to address this issue, Baddeley (2000), proposed that the working memory system has a limited capacity episodic buffer, which can bind information across the different sub-systems and integrate it with information from long-term memory.

Application to real life- Baddeley (1991) found that Alzheimer's patients had problems carrying out visual and verbal tasks at the same time. This is in contrast to 'normally functioning' people who can usually carry out different types of task at the same time easily. Baddeley suggested that the Alzheimer's patients had decreased central executive function and so they couldn't coordinate information from the different sub-systems within their working memory. Understanding why Alzheimer's patients struggle with memory and thinking, could lead to possible treatments for them in the future.

You need to be able to describe and evaluate the multi-store model of memory (Atkinson and Shiffrin, 1968), including short- and long-term memory, and ideas about information processing, encoding, storage and retrieval, capacity and duration.

Description:

Atkinson and Shiffrin (1968, 1971) described memory as having separate stores. These are referred to as sensory memory, short-term memory (STM) and long-term memory (LTM). For information to go from your sensory memory to your STM, attention is needed. Information in the STM that is sufficiently rehearsed is coded into LTM. Information that is stored in the sensory memory is only stored for a fraction of a second. The STM holds plus or minus seven items or chunks of information and can last between 18 and 30 seconds. The capacity of LTM is unlimited and information can last a lifetime. LTM is a single store which means that everything is stored together and items are stored in the order in which they have been learnt. In STM, information is held in acoustic form while in LTM it is held in semantic form.

Evaluation:

Studies-Glanzer and Cunitz (1966) presented participants with a list of words and found that people remembered more words from the beginning (primacy effect) and the end of the list (recency effect) and the fewest words from the middle. This primacy and recency effect support the idea of a separate STM and LTM. Participants remember more words from the beginning of the word list because they have had time to rehearse them and put them into LTM and they remember more words from the end of the word list because they are still in STM. The words in the middle of the list are forgotten because they have not been rehearsed and they are no longer in STM.

Other evidence for the existence of a separate STM and LTM comes from case studies of brain damaged patients. One example is the case of HM who had difficulty forming new long term memories but his short term memory was relatively normal.

Explanation-The multi-store model of memory is too simplistic. It is now widely believed that both STM and LTM have several separate storage systems. Seitz and Schumann-Hengsteler found that a visual-spatial task would not interfere with someone's ability to do sums. This suggests that there are separate short-term memory systems to handle visual and verbal information. HM could remember new motor skills and past information, suggesting that there are separate stores for LTM (facts, events, skills stores).

Application to real life-The concept of a separate STM and LTM is useful in helping psychologists think about memory. The multi-store model of memory helps to explain some of the memory problems with anterograde amnesia as people with this type of amnesia cannot form new long-term memories although they still have old memories and their STM is intact e.g. Clive Wearing.

You need to be able to describe and evaluate Tulving's (1972) explanation of long-term memory: Episodic and semantic memory

Description:

Episodic memory is a record of the episodes/experiences in our lives. As the events that have happened in our lives are linked to the time when they occurred, they are time-referenced. Retrieval of episodic memories is also dependent on recalling the context of the situation. Semantic memory is our general knowledge store and holds factual information. The time when we learnt the information is not important so semantic memories are not time-referenced. However, fragments of information in semantic memory can be pieced together so that they are in a temporal form. For example, we might learn about Roman times separately from the Middle Ages but we can then understand that the Middle Ages occurred at a later time. Retrieval of semantic memories is not dependent on context as we do not need to recall the context of when we learnt factual information to remember it. Semantic memory is unlikely to change when we recall facts because it is independent of context. In contrast, when we recall experiences from our lives and reflect on them within context, they are likely to be transformed.

Evaluation:

Studies-Case studies of amnesic patients have been used to support the distinction between episodic and semantic memory. Tulving argued that people with amnesia suffer from problems with episodic memory combined with an intact semantic memory. The case study of KC (1951-2014), who could not recall many personal events in his life but could learn new facts supports the idea of separate memory systems. Ostergaard (1987) described the case of a 10-year-old boy who had problems with his episodic memory but who was still able to learn new things. It was concluded that he was able to store information in his semantic memory. This study supports the idea that there are separate episodic and semantic memory systems. However, this boy did have some deficits in his semantic memory too. Cermak and O'Connor (1983) reported the case of an amnesic patient who could read a factual article on laser technology and discuss it at the time but who could not remember anything about it later. This suggests that he had deficits in both semantic and episodic memory. Therefore, some case studies of amnesic patients do not support a distinction between episodic and semantic memory as deficits are observed across both types of memory.

Case studies of brain-damaged patients suggest that long-term memory consists of more than episodic memory and semantic memory. Clive Wearing, a musician, could not remember episodes in his life but could remember how to play the piano. This case study suggests that there is different long-term memory store for practised skills. The term 'procedural memory' has been used to describe our memory for practised skills such as riding a bicycle. The case study of HM also supports the idea of a long-term memory store for practised skills. HM could learn new skills but could not remember learning them. For example, HM would get quicker at completing jigsaw puzzles even though he couldn't recall doing them.

Explanation-A criticism of Tulving's idea of separate episodic and semantic memory systems is that there needs to be communication between the systems. Episodic memory cannot work without semantic memory because in order to understand episodes in our lives we need to relate it to our general knowledge. Anderson and Ross (1980) found that semantic memory is also affected by episodic memory. They asked participants to decide whether a sentence was true or false, a test of semantic memory, and the results showed that their ability to verify the sentences was affected by prior episodic information. Such evidence suggests that episodic and semantic memory are not separate. Semantic memories may form through an abstraction of information from episodic memories.

Application to real life-Tulving's idea of episodic memory as being context dependent can explain why people forget information in the absence of the right cues (cue-dependent forgetting). The police often use cues during interviewing to reinstate the context of an incident to improve witness' memory of events.

You need to be able to describe and evaluate reconstructive memory (Bartlett, 1932)

Description:

Bartlett suggested that memory is an imaginative reconstruction of past events. We do not remember information accurately like a DVD recording but instead we are influenced by our prior knowledge. Schemas are 'packets of information' we have about the world and they affect how we interpret events. For example, we might have classroom schema and that might include the idea of a teacher, a whiteboard and some students being taught. If we are shown a film of a classroom situation, we might recall that the students were set homework even though they weren't because homework forms part of our classroom schema. When we retrieve stored memories, we use previous experiences to interpret the information and so the information is reconstructed. If there are any gaps in our memory, we may use schema to organise the information. Therefore, schemas may lead us to distort unfamiliar information so that it fits in with our existing knowledge.

Evaluation:

Studies- Bartlett carried out a number of repeated reproduction experiments to show that participants will reconstruct their memories. The repeated reproduction method involved participants being asked to recall a story or object after increasing time intervals. For example, in his 'War of the Ghosts' study, participants read the story twice and were then asked to recall it after several minutes, weeks, months and then years. Bartlett used eight unfamiliar stories altogether and a number of different pictures as well. He found that participants' memories were distorted. When participants were asked to recall the stories, they often shortened the stories and made them more coherent.

Explanation- Bartlett focused on memory being reconstructed at recall. However, our schema may also affect the way we perceive and understand information before it is stored. We may not store information exactly as it is presented to us but in a way that it makes sense to us. Bartlett may also have overemphasised the inaccuracy of our memory. Research into flashbulb memory has shown that we can remember emotionally significant events very accurately.

Application to real life-The concept of reconstructive memory has been used to explain why eyewitness testimony can be inaccurate. Innocent people have been convicted on the basis of eyewitness testimony alone and later been found innocent based on DNA evidence.

You need to be able to describe and evaluate the classic study Baddeley (1966b) 'The influence of acoustic and semantic similarity on long-term memory for word sequences'

Description:

Aim: To see whether words that sound similar (acoustically similar) or are similar in meaning (semantically similar) affect participants' ability to recall them in order (sequential recall).

Procedure: Male and female participants were divided into four conditions: In condition 1, they had to recall a list of acoustically similar words; in condition 2, they had to recall a list of acoustically dissimilar words; in condition 3, they had to recall a list of semantically similar words and in condition 4, they had to recall a list of semantically dissimilar words. Each list had 10 words and each word was displayed via a projector to the participants for a few seconds. Participants were then asked to remember some numbers to remove the words from their short-term memory. Then to test participants' sequential recall for their list of words, they were shown the words and asked to write them down in the order they had been presented. This was repeated four times. Participants were then given a 15 minute interference task where they had to copy some number sequences. Finally, participants were asked to recall their word list in order again to test their long-term memory for the words.

Results: Participants' sequential recall of semantically similar words was significantly worse than for semantically dissimilar words during the final stage of the experiment. Participants' sequential recall of acoustically similar words was not significantly different to acoustically dissimilar words during the final stage. However, initially participants' memory for the acoustically similar sounding words was worse compared to the acoustically dissimilar words.

Conclusion: It was difficult for participants to recall semantically similar words during the final stage as information is encoded in long-term memory semantically. Sequential recall of the acoustically similar words was worse at the beginning because information is encoded in short-term memory acoustically.

Evaluation:

Generalisability-Participants were all undergraduate students so were not representative of the wider population as they may have been more used to learning and recalling information.

Reliability-The study was conducted under controlled conditions and followed a standardised procedure. This makes the study easy to replicate and the reliability of the study can be tested. Studies that are reliable are considered more scientific.

Application to real life-The study suggests that information is encoded into short-term memory and long-term memory differently and so supports the idea of separate stores. This helps us to understand case studies of brain-damaged patients and why they have problems remembering some things but not others.

Validity-The study lacks ecological validity because the situation was artificial and does not relate to how we use memory in everyday life. The task lacked mundane realism as people are not usually asked to learn and recall a list of words. Furthermore, participants were asked to rehearse the words during four trials, which may have enhanced their memory for the words and is unlike how we remember things in real life.
Songs can be encoded in LTM without people thinking about their meaning, which suggests that some information in LTM can be encoded acoustically.

Ethics-There are no ethical issues so you don't need to comment on the ethics of this study at all.

You need to be able to discuss individual differences in memory including processing speed and schemas

People process information at different speeds. Some people can take longer to take in information than others. Children who have a slower 'processing speed' can get extra time in examinations to allow them process what they are being asked to do. There can also be individual differences in memory capacity. Sebastien and Hernandez-Gil (2012) found that younger children had shorter digit spans than older children.

Individuals may have slightly different schemas (packets of information) about the world. For example, one person's idea about what a criminal looks like may be different to another person's. Our perceptions can affect our outlook on a situation and also how we recall information. It has been shown that stereotypes can affect a witness' recall of a crime incident.

You need to be able to discuss individual differences in autobiographical memory

Autobiographical memory is our memory for the events that have happened during our lives. Our clearest memories tend to be recent ones or ones that occurred between 15 and 25-years-old (the reminiscence bump). It has been argued that we remember things well from our teenage years and early twenties because it is when we form our identity. Palombo et al. (2012) found individual differences in autobiographical memory. They questioned people about different aspects of their memory including episodic memory (memory for events) and semantic memory (memory for facts). They found that people who had poor episodic memories also had poor semantic memories. This suggests that the different types of memory are interlinked.

You need to be able to discuss how dyslexia affects children's memory, span and working memory (one area of developmental psychology)

Dyslexia is a developmental disorder that affects the way a person processes written material. People with dyslexia read at a level lower than would be expected for the age and intelligence. There is often a discrepancy between their oral and written abilities.

Dyslexia affects up to 10% of the population. More boys are affected than girls. Research has found the children with dyslexia have problems recognising similar sounding words (the phonological similarity effect). They also find it harder to remember strings of longer words relative to shorter words (the word length effect). This suggests that children with dyslexia have a poor verbal short-term memory.

Breznitz (2008) argues that dyslexia is caused by slow processing during the decoding of words. Breznitz and Horowitz (2007) found that children with dyslexia could be trained to process information at a faster speed.
However, there is still no universally accepted explanation of what constitutes dyslexia as there are wide variations in symptoms. It seems to have a genetic basis and it may be a neurological syndrome. Stein (2008) found that the development of magnocellular neurones is impaired in children with dyslexia. Furthermore, dyslexia can coincide with other learning difficulties such as attention hyperactivity disorder (ADHD) suggesting it is more than just a phonological issue.

The most effective intervention programmes in schools seem to focus on phonological awareness. Children with poor phonological awareness may not understand that if you change the letter 'c' in the word 'cat' to 'h', the word would become 'hat'.

Practising phoneme deletion is one technique that can improve dyslexic children's phonological awareness. For example, a teacher might use two cards with the word 'mice' on one and 'ice' on the other. They might then ask the child, 'If you take away 'm' from the word mice, what is left then?' Another technique is phoneme identification. For example, the teacher might say a single speech sound such as 't' and show six pictured words. The child then has to pick the picture that begins with 't'. Phoneme discrimination is another method of helping children with dyslexia to really listen to speech sounds. This is when two pictures of similar sounding words are presented together such as 'cat' and 'hat'. The teacher would then say such just one of the words and the child has to pick the correct picture.

Retgvoort and van der Leij (2007) used a 14 week home- and computer-based training in phonemic awareness and letter-sound relationships with children who were genetically at risk of dyslexia. Initially, the trained at-risk children kept up with untrained not-at-risk controls in reading ability. However, once the children started school, the trained at-risk children had delayed reading relative to the not-at-risk control children. This study shows the importance of support at school as well as at home and how the advantages of early intervention can be undone unless on-going help is provided.

You need to be able to describe and evaluate one contemporary study in cognitive psychology. For example, Steyvers and Hemmer (2012) 'Reconstruction from memory in naturalistic environments'

Description:

Aim-To see whether there is a link between episodic memory (memory for events) and semantic memory (memory for objects and facts) in everyday, natural environments. They wanted to see how prior knowledge (semantic memory) was used to reconstruct memory for photographs of normal everyday settings (episodic recall).

Procedure-The researchers found 25 images of everyday scenes. There were 5 types of scenes: kitchens, dining rooms, offices, hotels and urban scenes. 5 images were chosen of each of the 5 scene types.

The researchers wanted to find out what people might expect to see in a particular scene so 22 participants from the University of California were asked to list objects that might be in a kitchen, dining room, office, hotel and urban scene. As participants were asked to say what they expected to be in a scene, this was called the expectation test. In this condition, the participants were not shown any stimulus image.

25 other participants were shown the 5 scenes and asked to name any objects they could see. This was to check whether the people could see all the objects in the photographs that the researchers had placed there. This was called the perception test as it was used to check what participants could perceive.

In the main experiment, a separate group of 49 participants were shown a set of 5 images (there were 2 sets of 5 images altogether). The participants saw the images for either 2 seconds or 10 seconds and this was chosen randomly. For example, one participant might be allocated the following timings: Urban 10s, Office 10s, Dining 10s, Kitchen 2s, Hotel 2s. The participants were then asked to free recall all the objects that they could remember. The researchers believed that when participants only saw a scene for 2s, they would have to rely on prior knowledge (semantic knowledge) to help them recall it. In contrast, they believed that when participants saw the scene for 10s then they could use their episodic memory to recall the scene and would be better able to recall unusual objects in the scene.

The effect of prior knowledge (semantic memory) on recall was also tested by comparing participants' recall of the objects in the 2s and 10s conditions with the expectation test.

Results-The mean number of objects recalled when participants saw a scene for 2 seconds was 7.75 compared to 10.05 when participants had seen a scene for 10 seconds. Participants made very few errors in their recall. Incorrect recall of objects that would be expected to be in such as scene was only 9%. Incorrect recall of low probability objects was 18%, which suggests that participants were reasonably good at recalling unusual items.

Participants were able to guess many of the objects using prior knowledge (semantic memory). More than 55% of accurate object guesses were based on semantic memory. Participants were able to recall 80% of the objects in the 2s and 10s conditions, suggesting that episodic memory helped them to recall the rest of the objects.

Conclusion-Memory of naturalistic scenes can be accurate and reliable. Prior knowledge (semantic memory) can enhance recall.

Evaluation:

Generalisability-All the participants were university students, who are not representative of the wider population. However, as the study was looking at memory, which is similar across the general population except for the very young or very old, it could be deemed to be generalisable.

Reliability-The study had a clear standardised procedure with good controls. For example, the participants saw the photos for a certain amount of time under controlled conditions. The researchers could then compare recall in the 2s and 10s conditions fairly. Participants also only viewed one image of any scene such as the kitchen scene to make sure that photos of the same scene did not interfere with recall. These controls make the study replicable and reliable.

Application to real life-The study suggests that eyewitness memory is real life may be better than previous laboratory research has shown. Prior knowledge (semantic memory) may actually enhance recall and allow people to notice unusual features of the situation.

Validity-The study presented naturalistic scenes to participants, which enhances the ecological validity of the study. However, the study was still a laboratory experiment and involved an artificial situation. Seeing photographs of a scene is not the same as seeing it in real life.

Ethics-No ethical issues so no there is no need to discuss this.

An alternative contemporary study you could learn is Sebastián and Hernández-Gil's (2012) study of the developmental pattern of digit span

Description

Aim-To see whether digit span (a measure of phonological capacity) increases with age. To investigate whether there are any differences in digit span in Spanish culture compared to Anglo-Saxon culture. To compare digit span in children between 5- and 17-years-old and adults, older people and patients with dementia.

Procedure-570 participants were recruited from Madrid schools. All the participants were Spanish and between 5- and 17-years old. They were selected by school year and their cognitive functioning was controlled for. None of the participants had repeated a year and none of them had hearing, reading or writing difficulties. The participants were divided into five different age groups and they were all given a digit span test. Random sequences of digits were read aloud to participants at a rate of one digit per second. Initially, participants were given three sequences of three digits. Participants were then asked to recall the digits in the same order. The number of digits the participants had to recall increased each time by one digit. The digit span recorded for each participant was the maximum number of digits they could recall in the right order without any errors. The results were analysed by school year and by developmental period (5 years; 6-8 years; 9-11 years; 12-14 years and 15-17 years). Sebastián and Hernández-Gil also compared the data with results from their 2010 study looking at digit span amongst healthy older people and patients with Alzheimer's disease and frontotemporal dementia.

Results-Digit span increases with age from 3.76 at 5-years-old to 5.91 at 17-years-old. There was a steady increase in digit span with age amongst their Spanish participants. This contrasts with Anglo-Saxon research, which suggests that digit span does not increase past 15-years-old.

They also found that Spanish children's digit span was lower than Anglo-Saxon children of a comparable age.

When they compared the digit span of healthy older people (4.44) with those with Alzheimer's disease (4.20) and Frontotemporal dementia (4.22), they found a decreased digit span in all groups compared to the 17-year-olds. The healthy older people had a digit span of the average 7-year-old and the patients with Alzheimer's disease and Frontotemporal dementia had the digit span of the average 6-year-old. This suggests that the phonological loop is more affected by age than dementia.

Conclusion-Spanish digit words have more syllables e.g. cuatro, cinco, siete compared to English digit words e.g. four, five, six. Words with more syllables take longer to rehearse. This can explain why the Spanish children's digit span was lower than the Anglo-Saxon children of a comparable age.

Evaluation:

Generalisability-570 participants were used, which makes the sample representative of the wider Spanish population.

Reliability-The study had a standardised procedure involving participants being tested individually on their digit span under controlled conditions. This makes the study easy to repeat, which allows it to be tested for reliability.

Application to real life-Digit span can be used to make comparisons between individuals in terms of their verbal memory. This study shows that when comparisons are made using digit span, cultural differences should be accounted for.

Validity-The study lacks ecological validity because the situation was artificial. The task also lacked mundane realism. People are not usually asked to learn a list of digits in everyday life. Furthermore, testing participants' digit span may not be a good way of understanding how verbal memory is used in real situations.

However, the experiment has internal validity. Digit span tests have been shown to be a good indicator of reading ability, which relates to verbal memory.

Ethics-There are no ethical issues with this study so there is no need to discuss this.

You need to be able to discuss case studies of brain-damaged patients, including Henry Molaison (HM) and the use of qualitative data, including strengths and weaknesses of the case study as a research method

Cognitive neuropsychology studies brain-damaged patients to understand how the damage affects their behaviour and cognitive processes such as object recognition, memory and problem solving. Cognitive neuropsychologists use this information to understand how the brain works. For example, some brain-damaged patients have problems remembering information beyond 30 seconds. This provides support for the idea that we have a separate short- and long-term memory.

Henry Molaison (HM) suffered from severe epilepsy. In order to stop his seizures, an operation was carried out to remove his hippocampus. This stopped his seizures but led to damage to his long term memory. HM could remember items for a few minutes but not for long periods of time. This suggests a dissociation between two types of memory and supports Atkinson and Schiffrin's (1968) theory of a separate short-term memory (STM) and long-term memory (LTM) stores. However, a single dissociation does not provide enough evidence for separate memory stores as an alternative theory of HM's deficits would be that more effort is required to retain information for longer periods of time. On the other hand, the contrasting case of KF when looked at beside HM's case study provides further support for the idea of a separate short- and long-term memory. In contrast to HM, KF had impaired STM but his LTM was normal. The double dissociation shown by HM and KF provides support for Atkinson and Schiffrin's multi-store model of memory and the idea of a separate STM and LTM. However, although KF had a severely impaired STM, KF was able to perform a large range of cognitive tasks and had no problems understanding spoken language (Shallice and Warrington, 1970). This challenges the idea of a single STM store and led Baddeley and Hitch (1974) to develop a multi-component working memory model. The working memory model suggests that KF only had damage to the phonological loop component of his working memory and so although he had an auditory digit span of only two items, his visuo-spatial sketchpad and central executive were intact allowing him to process information.

Case studies of brain damaged patients include interviews with them about their experiences. The case studies also include description of how the amnesia has affected the patients' abilities and memory. For example, patients with anterograde amnesia report problems forming new memories and patients with retrograde amnesia have problems recalling past events. This means that qualitative data (descriptive data in words) is collected.

Evaluation:

Single case studies have contributed to our understanding of cognitive processes but they do have limitations. Brain-damaged patients may not be representative of the normal population so neuropsychologists need to be careful about making inferences about intact cognitive processes from such case studies. If brain damage occurs in early childhood, the brain can show plasticity and the damage can have different consequences for the patient. Bates (1998) found that babies who had suffered severe strokes to their left hemisphere could sometimes develop language processing in their right hemisphere.

There are also strengths and weaknesses of the qualitative data collected from case studies. Qualitative data can give rich, detailed information about brain-damaged patients' experiences and functioning. Such data is often considered more valid. However, qualitative data is harder to replicate and can lack reliability. Interpretation of qualitative can be subjective, and therefore, unscientific.

You need to be able to discuss a key question in the cognitive approach. One possible key question 'How can knowledge of working memory be used to inform the treatment of dyslexia?

Dyslexia is a developmental disorder that affects the way a person processes written material. People with dyslexia read at a level lower than would be expected for the age and intelligence. There is often a discrepancy between their oral and written abilities.

Children with dyslexia have problems recognising similar sounding words (the phonological similarity effect) suggesting they have deficits in the phonological loop component of their working memory. They also find it harder to remember strings of longer words relative to shorter words (the word length effect). This suggests that children with dyslexia have a poor verbal short-term memory. A key question is whether knowing about working memory can help children with dyslexia.

The concept of working memory can be helpful in understanding the difficulties that children with dyslexia face. Working memory is important in reading and understanding words and so deficits in working memory can lead to the problems in these areas. Many children with dyslexia can also have difficulties with following a sequence of instructions and focusing their attention. This can be understood through them having a low working memory capacity. Children's performance at school is likely to be affected by these problems so it is important to provide suitable interventions so that they can achieve their full potential.

Loosli et al. (2011) used a computer-based working memory training programme with 9- to 11-year-old typically developing children and found that they had significantly enhanced reading performance after training compared to a control group. This study supports the idea that working memory is involved in reading ability. Dunning et al. (2012) also found that practising memory tasks on a computer could improve verbal working memory.

Alloway used a training programmed to develop children's working memory. The found that children who practised memory skills four times a week for 30 minutes had higher IQ and working memory scores compared to those who only practised once a week or not at all. When she followed them up 8 months later, they still showed the same improvements in grades, working memory, and IQ.

Breznitz (2008) argues that dyslexia is caused by slow processing during the decoding of words. This may be because their working memory has a low capacity. Breznitz and Horowitz (2007) found that children with dyslexia could be trained to process information at a faster speed.

Understanding that children with dyslexia may find it difficult to do a number of different things at the same time can inform teaching practice. For example, teachers should avoid talking and explaining concepts whilst the students are making notes. Tasks should also be broken down into smaller steps so that students' working memory is not overloaded with instructions.

Some of the most effective intervention programmes in schools seem to focus on phonological awareness. Children with poor phonological awareness may not understand that if you change the letter 'c' in the word 'cat' to 'h', the word would become 'hat'. This may because children need strategies to overcome deficits with the phonological loop component of their working memory.

Retgvoort and van der Leij (2007) used a 14 week home- and computer-based training in phonemic awareness and letter-sound relationships with children who were genetically at risk of dyslexia. They found that the trained at-risk children kept up with untrained not-at-risk controls in reading ability short-term.

Alternative key question: 'Is eyewitness testimony reliable?'

Eyewitness testimony refers to the recalled memory of a witness to a crime or incident. Innocent people have been convicted on the basis of eyewitness testimony alone and have later been found innocent using DNA evidence. Cases like this call into question the reliability of eyewitness testimony. There is also the issue that juries tend to trust eyewitness testimony perhaps disproportionately.

Eyewitness Testimony is unreliable because:

Witnesses' memories for events are not accurate video recordings but subject to errors. If witnesses have gaps in their memory, they may use schema to reconstruct their memories. Schemas may also influence the way a memory is encoded.

Leading questions can influence eyewitness memory and produce errors in recall. Loftus and Palmer (1974) found that they could affect participants recall by changing the way a question is worded. Participants were asked how fast a car was going when it 'hit', 'smashed', 'collided' or 'bumped'. Participants gave a higher estimate of speed if the word was 'smashed' rather than 'collided', they were also more likely to report seeing broken glass in the 'smashed' condition when asked back a week later.

Weapon focus effect: Studies show that when a weapon is used by a criminal, witnesses focus on the weapon rather than the criminal's face or their environment, probably because a weapon is a major threat. Loftus et al. (1987) showed half their participants a film with a customer in a restaurant holding a cheque, and the other half were shown a film with a customer holding a gun. They found that participants had worse recall for a the customer's face when they were holding a weapon.

Yarmey's (2004) study supports the view that jurors should question the reliability of witness identification from line-ups. They found that when participants had actually spoken to a female target, only 49% of them could identify her in a photo line-up when she was present and when she was not present 38% of them decided than one of the filler photos was the target.

Poor line-up procedures may lead to misidentification of a suspect. Simultaneous line-ups (where all the people are presented together in the line-up) may lead to witnesses using a relative judgement strategy (choosing a person who looks most like the perpetrator of the crime rather than really looking at the person's individual characteristics to see whether they match up).

Meissner and Brigham (2001) found that people are less able to recognise people from a different ethnic background to them so this can lead to problems in eyewitness identification.

Buckout (1974) highlighted that photo line-ups can be biased if the suspect's photo is physically different from the fillers.

Busey and Loftus (2006) pointed out that lack of double-blind procedures can mislead witnesses. They gave the example of a police officer who knew who the suspect was in a line-up and when a witness identified the suspect, the police officer said sign here as if to confirm their identification was correct.

Wells and Bradfield found that if a participant was given confirming feedback about an identification they became more confident that their identification was correct. Therefore, by the time a case gets to court, a witness who has had their identification confirmed by a police officer, may be overly confident even if they are wrong.

If there is a long period of time between recall and the incident, people are likely to forget details.

Stereotypes can affect eyewitness memory. People's views on what type of person commits a crime can affect recall. People are less likely to believe that a man is a suit committed a crime compared to someone who is scruffily dressed.

The memory conformity effect can affect witnesses' memory for events. For example, if witnesses discuss a crime incident together, their memory for events becomes more similar. Wright et al. (2000) placed people in pairs to investigate the memory conformity effect under controlled conditions. One of the pair saw pictures of a man entering with the thief, the other saw pictures without the man. They were then asked to recount the story together but fill out questionnaires separately. About half of the participants who had not seen the picture with the man conformed to their partner's account.

Eyewitness Testimony is reliable because:

Yuille and Cutshall (1986) examined the recall of witnesses to a real life gun shooting in Canada. 21 witnesses saw a man try to rob a gun shop and then shoot the shop owner. The shop owner shot back and killed the thief. After the witnesses had been interviewed by police, the researcher used the opportunity to ask them whether they would like to take part in their research into eyewitness testimony. 13 of the 21 witnesses agreed to take part in their research 5 months later. They found that even 5 months after the incident, witnesses had good recall of events and were not affected by the leading questions asked. This study suggests that eyewitness memory in real life is not as likely to be distorted as laboratory experiments suggest.

Rinolo et al. (2003) questioned 20 survivors of the shipwrecked Titanic shipwreck and found that 15 of the 20 witnesses were able to recall details accurately many years later despite inaccurate media coverage.

Cognitive interviews can improve eyewitness testimony: this involves getting the witness to freely describe events without the risk of leading questions. Eyewitnesses are asked to not leave out any detail even if they think it is unimportant and they may be asked to recall the incident in reverse order. Questions can be asked at the end in order for information to be un-altered.

Flashbulb memory may lead witnesses to recall crime incidents very clearly as they are likely to have strong emotions related to the incident and may replay events in their mind.

You need to be able to describe and evaluate the laboratory, field and natural experiments

Laboratory Experiments involve manipulating an independent variable to see the effects on a dependent variable. The dependent variable is measured. Extraneous variables are controlled so that a cause and effect relationship can be established.

Evaluation:

Laboratory experiments have standardised procedures and good controls. This makes them easily replicable and reliable. They can establish cause and effect. However, laboratory experiments lack ecological validity as they are carried out in artificial situations and often involve artificial tasks.

Field experiments looks at participants in their natural environment whilst manipulating the independent variable. The dependent variable is measured. As field experiments take place in a natural environment, extraneous variables are hard to control.

Evaluation:

Field experiments take place in the participants' natural environment. This means that not all the extraneous variables can be controlled and the findings might not be reliable. However, as field experiments have carefully controlled and planned procedures, they often give the same results when repeated. This means that they can be as reliable as laboratory experiments. Field experiments are carried out in the participants' natural environment so they have ecological validity in terms of setting. However, the independent variable(s) is still carefully manipulated to see the effect on the dependent variable, and therefore, the procedure may not be valid. On the other hand, researchers try to make the procedure as realistic as possible to enhance validity.

Natural Experiments are studies carried out in real-life setting where the independent variable occurs naturally. A dependent variable is still measured. Participants cannot be allocated to conditions so it is not a true experiment.

Evaluation:
Natural experiments have high ecological validity as they are carried out in participants' natural environments. However, it can be difficult to establish cause and effect as the extraneous variables are not controlled.

You need to be able to discuss how quantitative data is obtained from experiments

Experiments involve measuring a dependent variable such a number of words recalled, speed estimates and number of aggressive behaviours shown. This is quantitative data, which can be statistically analysed to see how significant the results are or whether they may be due to chance. If quantitative research is repeated, often the same data will be found. This shows that quantitative data is reliable. However, the careful operationalising of variables in quantitative research means that real life events and interactions are not being measured so there can be a problem with validity.

You need to understand and be able to write one-tailed, two-tailed and null hypotheses

An experimental hypothesis predicts what change(s) will take place in the dependent variable when the independent variable is manipulated.

A two-tailed (non-directional) hypothesis predicts that there will be a change in the DV when the IV is manipulated.
e.g. There will be a difference in the number of words recalled when words are processed semantically compared to when they are processed phonetically.

A one-tailed (directional) hypothesis predicts in which direction the change will take place.
e.g. There will be more words recalled when they are processed semantically compared to when they are processed phonetically.

The null hypothesis states that there will be no changes due to the manipulation of the IV.
e.g. There will be no difference in the number of words recalled when processed semantically or phonetically.

Operationalisation: When you operationalise a hypothesis you make it clear what you are going to measure. Try and refer to something numerical. For example, if you are measuring recall, you might say number of words recalled.

You need to be able to describe and evaluate different types of design. You need to be to describe order effects, counterbalancing and randomisation in relation to the repeated measures design

An independent groups design involves testing separate groups of participants. Each group is tested in a different condition. For example, a researcher might ask one group to process words semantically and a second group to process words phonetically.

Advantages: An independent groups design avoids order effects. Each participant only takes part in one condition so they are less likely to become bored and tired (a fatigue effect) and less likely to become practiced at the task (a practice effect). There is also less likelihood of demand characteristics (where the participant guesses the aim of the study and changes their behaviour to please the experimenter) as they do only one condition.

Disadvantages: More people are needed than with the repeated measures design. Differences between participants in the groups may affect results, for example; variations in age, sex or social background. These differences are known as participant variables.

A repeated measures design involves testing the same group of people in different conditions. For example, the same group of people might be asked to process words semantically and phonetically.

Advantages: A repeated measures design avoids the problem of participant variables as the same participants do all conditions. Fewer people are needed.

Disadvantages: There are more likely to be demand characteristics as participants might guess the aim of the study as they take as they take part in more than one condition of the experiment.

Order effects are also more likely to occur with a repeated measures design. There are two types of order effects: practice effects and fatigue effects. Practice effects are when participants become better at a task such as learning a list of words in the second condition compared to the first condition. Fatigue effects are when participants might become bored or tired in the second condition.

Counterbalancing can overcome order effects in a repeated measured design. Counterbalancing is when the experimenter alters the order in which participants perform the different conditions of an experiment. For example, group 1 does condition A first then condition B, group 2 does condition B first then condition A.

Randomisation can overcome order effects as well. Randomisation is when the experimenter asks the participants to carry out the different conditions of the experiment in a random order.

A matched pairs design involves testing separate groups of people who are matched on certain characteristics. For example, each member of one group is same age, gender, race and or socioeconomic status as a member of the other group.

Advantages: A matched pairs design overcomes some of the problems of both an independent groups design and a repeated measures design. As the participants in the different conditions are matched, there is a reduced chance of participant variables affecting the results unlike an independent groups design. A matched pairs design also avoids the problem of order effects as there are different participants in each condition.

Disadvantages: A matched pairs design can be very time-consuming as the researcher need find closely matched pairs of participants. It is also impossible to match people exactly.

You need to be able to describe operationalisation of variables, extraneous variables and confounding variables

Operationalisation of variables refers to clearly defining what your independent and dependent variables are. For example, if you are investigating whether cues affect memory, you need to explain what type of cue you are looking at and how you will measure memory. In this example, the independent variable might be 'Whether participants are in the same room or a not when learning and recalling a list of words' and the dependent variable might be 'number of words recalled from a list of 20 words'.

Extraneous variables are are unwanted variables that can influence the results of an experiment.

Confounding variables are extraneous variables which affect the results of the experiment to the extent that you can't clearly see how the independent variable has affected the dependent variable. For example, a researcher may want to investigate whether mindmaps or flashcards are better at aiding recall of unfamiliar material such as Arabic. A confounding variable in this experiment would be if some of participants were already familiar with Arabic.

You need to be able to describe situation and participant variables

Situation variables and participant variables are types of extraneous variable.

Situation variables are environmental differences such as temperature, noise, other people etc. that can affect how participants respond in an experiment. For example, if an experiment is carried out over a number of days and one of the days there is a lot of noise from building work, this could affect participants' responses.

Participant variables are individual differences between participants, in terms of intelligence, mood, anxiety levels, age, IQ etc. For example, a policeman might be able to judge the speed of a car much better than a young student with no driving experience.

You need to be able to discuss objectivity, reliability and validity (internal, predictive and ecological)

Objectivity

An experiment is more likely to be objective if the data is collected in a strictly controlled environment. Quantitative (numerical) data is less open to interpretation than qualitative (descriptive) data and is viewed as more objective. Such data is also viewed as more credible, reliable and scientific.

Validity

A study has **internal validity** when the material or procedures used in the research measured what they were supposed to measure. For example, if an experimenter uses digit span to measure verbal memory and it has been found that digit span is a good indicator of this, then the study has internal validity.
Studies that avoid demand characteristics and experimenter effects have good internal validity.

A study has **predictive validity** if it accurately predicts a result in the future. For example, ALIS tests have predictive validity if they are good at predicting who will perform well at A-level.

A study has **ecological validity** if it is done in participants' natural environment and involves a situation that they might experience in real life. For example, if you get participants to come to a university and learn lists of words as test of memory, then you are not capturing how memory is used in real life and the study will lack ecological validity.

When discussing ecological validity you may also want to talk about mundane realism. If the study involves an artificial task like learning a list of words in two minutes, the study lacks mundane realism.

Reliability

If a study has a standardised procedure and was done under controlled conditions, then it is easy to replicate. A study is reliable if it has been replicated and similar results have been found. For example, if students are given an ALIS test on two different occasions and their results are similar, then the test can be seen as reliable.

You need to be able to describe experimenter effects and demand characteristics

Participants may try to guess what a psychological experiment is about. Demand characteristics refer to when participants change their behaviour based on what they think the experimenter wants to find from the research. In order to avoid demand characteristics, participants are sometimes not told they are in an experiment or they may be deceived about the true aims of the study (a single-blind experiment).

Experimenters can affect the behaviour of their participants and the results of their study. This is called experimenter effects. For example, the researcher might unwittingly communicate his expectations to the participants. Researchers can also interpret data in a biased way to match their expectations. To avoid experimenter effects, an experimenter may ask another researcher who doesn't know the aim of the study to carry out the actual experiment on participants (a double-blind procedure).

You need to be able to discuss control issues with experiments

One way an experiment can be controlled is through standardisation. This is when an experiment is set up so that all participants experience exactly the same procedure. For example, participants are given exactly the same instructions and carry out the tasks they have been given under the same controlled conditions. The only difference that participants may experience is the manipulation of the independent variable.

You need to understand when to use the inferential tests

One problem with the mean is that it doesn't tell you whether the difference between two conditions is significant or not. For example, you might do an experiment to test whether cues affect recall and your results show that the mean number of words recalled with a cue is 11.2 and the mean number of words recalled without a cue is 12.3. These figures suggest that the participants can recall more words with a cue and so you might conclude that cues do aid recall. However, it is difficult to judge whether the difference in the number of words recalled with a cue or without a cue is big enough to be certain of this conclusion. Perhaps on a different day or with different participants, you might have found less of a difference between the two conditions. An inferential test is a statistical test that shows you whether the difference between the two conditions is significant or not.

You choose an inferential test based on the design of the experiment and the level of data you collected.

You need to be able to recognise levels of data

Nominal data is made up of discrete categories. For example, you might categorise participants as either 'extroverts' or 'introverts'.

Ordinal data are ranked data. For example, you might rank participants on how well they recognise emotional expressions. Helen came first, Alex came second and Philippa came third.

Interval data are measurements along a scale with no true zero. For example, IQ can be measured along a scale but there is no true zero for IQ. Most people have an IQ between 70 and 130. For example, Helen has an IQ of 120, Alex has an IQ of 117 and Philippa has an IQ of 115.

Ratio data are measurements along a scale with a true zero. For example, time can be measured along a scale and there is a true zero. For example, Helen completed a spatial awareness task in 90s, Alex completed the task in 97s and Philippa completed the task in 105s.

You need to understand about probability and level of significance
($p \leq 0.10$ $p \leq 0.05$ $p \leq 0.01$)

In psychology, a significance level of $p \leq 0.05$ is chosen.

$p \leq 0.05$ means that there is an equal or less than 5% probability that the results could have occurred due to chance.

p = the probability of the results being due to chance

$\leq$ = less than or equal to

0.05 = 1 in 20 = 5%

Psychologists prefer to use the significance level: $p \leq 0.05$ to judge whether to accept a hypothesis or not. This means that there is an equal or less than 5% probability that the results are due to chance e.g. the group that received a cue recalled more words than the group that did not receive a cue and there is a less than 5% chance that the difference between the two groups could have been due to chance (random differences between the groups).

Sometimes researchers use the significance level: $p \leq 0.1$ to judge whether to accept a hypothesis or not. This means that there is an equal or less than 10% probability that the results are due to chance. You can see that this is less conservative than $p \leq 0.05$. It is easier for the hypothesis to be accepted even though the null hypothesis might be true. This leads to a type 1 error. Type 1 errors can lead to false positive results; accepting a hypothesis even though it is incorrect. This could lead to psychologists thinking that there is a significant difference between participant's recall when they are given a cue and not given a cue when there isn't a significant difference in recall.

Sometimes researchers use the significance level: $p \leq 0.01$ to judge whether to accept a hypothesis or not. This means that there is an equal or less than 1% probability that the results are due to chance. You can see that this is stricter than $p \leq 0.05$. It is harder for the hypothesis to be accepted even though it might actually be correct. This leads to a type 2 error. Type 2 errors can lead to false negative results; rejecting a hypothesis when it is correct. This could lead to psychologists thinking that there was no difference between participants recall when given a cue compared to no cue, when there was a significant difference.

You need to know when to use a Mann-Whitney U test and a Wilcoxon test and to understand what observed and critical values are

You use a Mann-Whitney U test when you have an independent groups design, ordinal data and you are testing for a difference between groups.

You use a Wilcoxon test when you have a repeated measures design, ordinal data and you are testing for a difference between conditions.

To decide whether the results are significant there must be an equal or less than 5% probability that the results are due to chance. If the results are significant, then psychologists say that they are rejecting the null hypothesis. In essence, they mean that they are accepting the experimental hypothesis but it is standard form to refer to rejecting the null hypothesis.

In order to decide whether the results are significant or not the observed value (the result obtained from the data collected) is compared to the critical value.

The critical value is a statistical 'cut-off' point. It is a number presented on a table of critical values that determines whether the result is significant enough for the null hypothesis not to be accepted.

The observed value relates to the data that has been collected in an experiment. You calculate an observed value by using the relevant formula for the statistical test you have decided to you use and inputting your collected data. The observed value that you calculate is compared with the relevant critical value to see if a null hypothesis should be rejected or not.

Note: You don't need to remember the formula of the Mann-Whitney U test or Wilcoxon as they will be given on your data sheet. However, you do need to understand how to input data into them and calculate an observed value.

At A2 you need to be able to use a Mann-Whitney U or Wilcoxon T Critical Values Table

In order to interpret the critical values tables, you need to know whether the hypothesis was one-tailed or two-tailed; the number of participants in each condition (shown as 'N' on the table) and the significance level. The values in the Mann-Whitney test are termed 'U' and the values in the Wilcoxon test are termed 'T'. Unlike the Spearman-rank and Chi-squared tests the observed value has to be equal to or less than the critical value for the results to be significant (i.e. to accept the experimental hypothesis and reject the null hypothesis).

You need to be able to describe a practical in the cognitive approach. Example practical: A dual task experiment to test the working memory model

Aim: To test the limited capacity of the phonological loop by carrying out a dual task experiment. To see whether carrying out two verbal tasks at the same time is harder than doing one verbal task and one visuo-spatial task.

One-tailed Hypothesis: Participants will recall fewer words from a list when they are asked to recite the song 'twinkle twinkle little star' than when they are asked to complete a puzzle.

Null Hypothesis: The number of words recalled will not be affected by whether participants are asked to do another verbal task or a visuo-spatial task.

Independent Variable: Type of task. Whether participants are asked to carry out a second verbal task or a visuo-spatial task.

Dependent Variable: The number of words recalled.

Sampling Method: Opportunity Sampling

Design: Independent Groups

Procedure:
20 participants were recruited using opportunity sampling due to the limited timescale. All the participants were from the sixth form and were over 16 years old. An independent measures design was employed and the participants were divided into two groups of ten. All the participants were told that they had to recall a list of twenty unrelated words. Group 1 was asked to recite 'Twinkle Twinkle Little Star' at the same time as learning the list of words. This was to see whether carrying out two verbal tasks at the same time would interfere with recall of the word list. The working memory model suggests that the phonological loop has limited capacity. Group 2 was asked to complete a twenty-four-piece puzzle of Thomas the tank engine (a visual spatial task) at the same time as learning the word list. The working memory model suggests that a visuo-spatial task should not interfere with a verbal task as it involves a different component of working memory. Standardised instructions were read to each participant and they were informed of their

right to withdraw from the study at any time. The experiment was carried out individually in a classroom. Participants were debriefed at the end of the experiment.

Results:

	Visuo-spatial task	Verbal task
Mean	12.4	9.9
Median	12	10.5
Mode	12	11
Range	6	5

Participants had a mean recall of 12.4 words when completing the puzzle a visuo-spatial task) compared to 9.9 words when reciting 'Twinkle Twinkle Little Star' (a verbal task).

Conclusion:
Two verbal tasks will interfere with each other more than a verbal task combined with a visuo-spatial task. This provides evidence for the different components of working memory.

Evaluation:

Generalisability: We used an opportunity sample of 16-17 year olds in our sixth form. Therefore, our sample is not representative of the wider population. However, as most people's cognitive abilities are similar, this study on memory could be considered generalisable.

Reliability: This experiment is reliable, because the extraneous variables were controlled and we used a standardised procedure. However, as an opportunity sample was used, it would be hard for someone else to obtain the same sample and repeat the findings making the study less reliable.

Validity: The experiment lacks ecological validity because learning and recalling a list of words is an artificial task.

Exemplar exam question:

Describe and evaluate one model of memory other than working memory. (12 marks)

Student answer:

The multi-store model of memory suggests there are three stores of information in the brain. Information is taken in by the senses and held briefly in the sensory store. Information is then either retained in short-term memory (STM) or is forgotten. The STM can hold up to 7 chunks of information for a short amount of time. The information is encoded by the way it was processed in the sensory store i.e. if it was seen it will remain as visual information. In the STM, information can encoded acoustically, visually or semantically. Information can then either be forgotten or retained in the long-term memory (LTM). In the LTM, the capacity is unlimited and the length of time it is held for is potentially unlimited also. The information can be encoded in any form. Information can be rehearsed by the rehearsal loop, which brings information into the STM from the LTM and back again.

The multi-store model of memory may be too simplistic. The working memory model describes short-term memory as an active store that holds and manipulates information consisting of the visuo-spatial sketchpad and the phonological loop. Tulving's theory of episodic and semantic memory suggests that there are different types of long-term memory too. This is backed up by case studies of brain-damaged patients who cannot form new long-term memories off episodes in their lives but can get better at practised skills. However, the multi-store model was a breakthrough into memory theories and led to research and theories that are now accepted today. It can be applied to real life as it suggests that we can only attempt to remember 7 chunks of information for a short time. This has been supported by studies as 7 chunks of random trigrams could be remembered as 7 chunks but not all in one go. Peterson and Peterson showed that information is encoded by the senses. They used a table of letters and found that participants could not recall the letters after being briefly shown them. The multi-store model does not explain cases such as Clive Wearing who has brain damage and extreme memory loss but can still remember how to play the piano.

6/12 marks

Commentary:

There is a reasonable description of the multi-store model of memory here. However, this student does not describe how information flows through the system. For information to go from sensory memory to STM, attention is needed. For information to go from STM to LTM, rehearsal is required. It can be helpful to draw a flow diagram in the exam. The description would also have benefited from a description of the capacity of each store. Information that is stored in the sensory memory is only stored for a fraction of a second whereas information in STM can last between 18 and 30 seconds. The capacity of LTM is unlimited and information can last a lifetime. There were a couple of errors in the description. The STM does not hold seven chunks of information but plus or minus 7 items or chunks. STM, information is held in acoustic form while in LTM it is held in semantic form. Information is encoded acoustically in STM not visually or semantically. Visual information is changed to sounds.

There is a reasonable attempt at an evaluation. There is a good comparison with the working memory model and Tulving's explanation of long-term memory. However, the Peterson and Peterson study has been mixed up with a different study. Peterson and Peterson (1959) investigated the duration of short-term memory using 3 consonant trigrams (e.g. MCR). Participants were asked to recall the trigrams after 3, 6, 9, 12, 15 or 18 seconds. They found that after a 3 second delay, 80% of the trigrams could be recalled but after an 18 second delay, less that 10% of the trigrams could be recalled. This study provides support for the limited duration of STM. The case study of Clive Wearing is not well explained. Clive Wearing has difficulty forming new long term memories but his short term memory is relatively normal. Therefore, the study supports the existence of a separate STM and LTM. However, the case study also highlights problems with the multi-store model of memory. Although Clive Wearing cannot remember a conversation he had 30 seconds ago, he can form new procedural memories. Procedural memory refers to the memory for performing certain kinds of tasks such as tying shoe laces or riding a bike. Procedural memories are usually automatically accessed. The multi-store model is too simplistic because it does not take into account different types of LTM such as procedural memory.

Chapter 3-Biological Psychology

You need to be able to describe what the biological approach is about

The biological approach is about how our genes, hormones and nervous system affect our behaviour.

You need to be able to describe how the central nervous system (CNS) and neurotransmitters affect human behaviour, including the structure and role of the neuron, the function of neurotransmitters and synaptic transmission

A Neuron: is a nerve cell. They send electrical messages, called nerve impulses, along their length.

A Synapse: is the tiny gap between two neurons. When a nerve impulse travels along a pre-synaptic neuron (a sending neuron), it triggers the nerve ending to release neurotransmitters across the synapse. The neurotransmitters diffuse across the synapse and bind with receptors on the post-synaptic neuron (the receiving neuron). This causes the post-synaptic neuron to transmit a nerve impulse.

Neurotransmitters: are chemical messengers that carry a signal across a synapse from one neuron to another. Examples of neurotransmitters are dopamine and serotonin.

Receptors: are sites on the post-synaptic neuron (the receiving neuron) that bind with neurotransmitters.

The central nervous system (CNS) consists of the brain and spinal cord. Sensory neurons are nerves that carry information from the sensory organs (such as our skin or ears) to the CNS. The brain processes this information and sends a message back to the motor neurons. These neurons then carry information to parts of our body to produce a response such as moving our leg. For example, if we see that the TV remote control is on the other side of the room, sensory neurons send this information to the CNS. The brain processes where the TV remote control is in the room and it sends a message to the parts of the body involved in movement.

Messages travel along neurons via nerve impulses (electrical impulses). The tiny gap between two neurons is called a synapse. When a nerve impulse travels along a pre-synaptic neuron (a sending neuron), it triggers the nerve ending to release neurotransmitters across the synapse. Neurotransmitters are chemicals messengers that carry a signal across a synapse from one neuron to another. Examples of neurotransmitters are dopamine and serotonin. The neurotransmitters diffuse across the synapse and bind with receptors on the post-synaptic neuron (the receiving neuron). This causes the post-synaptic neuron to transmit the message onwards via a nerve impulse.

Behaviour is strongly influenced by the nervous system. For example, high levels of serotonin, a neurotransmitter, make us feel happy. Low levels of serotonin are thought to reduce the ability to control aggressive impulses.

You need to be able to describe and evaluate the effect of recreational drugs on the transmission process in the central nervous system

Description:

Recreational drugs refer to substances that are taken for pleasure. These include legal drugs such as alcohol, caffeine and nicotine and illegal drugs such as cannabis, cocaine, heroin and ecstasy.

Nicotine affects the reward pathway in the brain. When a person smokes nicotine it binds to nicotinic receptors and excites the neuron leading to the release of dopamine into the synapse. Dopamine is related to feelings of pleasure so smoking nicotine can be addictive. However, increased dopamine in the synapse leads to over-stimulation of the dopamine receptors on the post-synaptic neuron and they can become damaged. When there are fewer dopamine receptors on the post-synaptic neuron, a person can become desensitised to the effects of dopamine. As a result, over time more nicotine is needed to produce the same pleasurable feelings. This is called tolerance and can lead to addiction. A person may need to take nicotine just to maintain the same levels of dopamine that were in the brain before they started taking it. Addiction is when person finds a drug so rewarding that they feel they must have it.

Cocaine also leads to an increase in dopamine and feelings of pleasure. It works by binding to the receptors on the pre-synaptic neuron stopping reuptake of dopamine. As a result, there is an excess of dopamine in the synapse. The post-synaptic dopamine receptors are over-stimulated by dopamine leading to feelings of pleasure. As with nicotine, the over-stimulation of the post-synaptic dopamine receptors can lead to damage and desensitisation. In turn, this causes tolerance and addiction.

Cannabis works by binding to cannabinoid receptors. This blocks the activity of the neurons in the hippocampus area of the brain. As the hippocampus is involved in memory, taking cannabis can lead to memory loss. Cannabis also leads to an increase in dopamine leading to feelings of pleasure. One explanation is that cannabis inhibits the GABA neurons, which then increases the activity of the dopamine neurons and releases more dopamine into the synapses in the reward pathway of the brain.

Evaluation:

Studies-Li et al. (2013) found that the brains of heroin addicts respond differently to heroin-related images compared to non-addicts. Heroin-related images can trigger activity in the PCC and other brain areas linked to rewards and cravings in heroin addicts. This study supports the theory that recreational drugs affect the dopamine reward system.

Explanation- The idea that recreational drugs affect dopamine levels in the reward area of the brain, leading to feelings of pleasure is supported by people's experiences of taking the drugs. This gives the theory face validity. Research also shows that people develop a tolerance to drugs over time and that they can become addicted. This supports the idea of the desensitising effect of recreational drugs.

However, it may be too simplistic to say that recreational drugs affect just dopamine levels in the brain and one reward pathway as the brain is complex.

Application to real life-Understanding how recreational drugs work can help health professionals in preventing drug use and helping those who are already drug users.

You need to be able to describe and evaluate how the structure of the brain, different brain areas (e.g. pre-frontal cortex) and brain functioning can be used to explain aggression as a human behaviour

Description:

The prefrontal cortex is involved in regulating emotions and behaviour. If a person's prefrontal cortex is damaged or dysfunctioning, they may not be able to regulate their anger and are more likely to show aggressive behaviour.

The limbic system is also associated with aggressive behaviour. It includes the amygdala and hypothalamus. The amygdala is believed to play an important role in aggression and the hypothalamus is involved in regulating our arousal levels (the fight or flight response).

Evaluation:

Studies- Phineas Gage was a railway worker whose brain was damaged in a railway accident. After the accident, he became much more aggressive. This suggests that certain parts of the brain are linked to aggression. However, this is a unique study and it is difficult to generalise the findings.

Bard (1940) lesioned the brains of cats and found that the hypothalamus and amygdala were responsible for aggression.
However, there are problems with generalising animal research to humans as humans are more complex. For example, the prefrontal cortex in animals is smaller than in humans.

Swantje et al. (2012) found that women with smaller amygdalas were more likely to have higher aggression scores. This supports the idea that the amygdala plays an important role in aggression.

Explanation-The idea that brain structure affects aggression has scientific credibility as brain scans (e.g. PET, MRI) show differences in brain activity in those who are particularly prone to aggression.

Application to real life-Understanding how brain structure affects aggression can be helpful in criminal cases. For example, Raine et al. found that murderers who were pleading not guilty due to reasons of insanity did have different levels of activity in the brain compared to non-murderers.

You need to be able to describe and evaluate the role of evolution and natural selection to explain behaviour, including aggression

Description:

Evolutionary psychology focuses on how humans have adapted to show certain behaviours through the process of natural selection. The theory of natural selection says that traits that aid our survival are more likely to be passed on through our genes.

For example, aggressive behaviour may have been an important behaviour in ensuring our survival amongst our ancestors so these traits are more likely to be passed down the generations. Females may have selected males who were more aggressive to provide greater protection for them and their offspring. Male aggression may have been driven by the desire to find a suitable partner. Aggression can be used to assert dominance and power amongst same sex rivals and females are said to be attracted to dominant and powerful men.

Evolutionary psychology can also explain the aggression as a response to sexual jealousy. People may behave aggressively out of the desire to keep their mate. For example, a person may be jealous of their partner flirting with a rival and respond with aggression. Some research suggests that men are more likely than women to use aggression against a rival.

Evaluation:

Studies-Buss and Shackleton (1997) found that men would try to intimidate other males if they felt their relationship was threatened. This supports the idea that men may use aggression to maintain their relationships with women and to ensure their genes are passed on.
Dobash and Dobash (1984) found that sexual jealousy could lead to violence against women. This suggests that male aggression may be a trait that has evolved to ensure survival of their genes.

Explanation-A limitation of the evolutionary explanation of aggression is that it does not explain why some people who are provoked will respond with aggression whereas others will not. Aggression may also be counter-productive in ensuring a person's survival. If a person is aggressive and gets into fights with other people, their behaviour may decrease their chance of survival.

Application to real life-If women notice mate retention strategies in their partners such as jealousy when they speak to other men, they may be at risk of violence and should be cautious about continuing the relationship.

You need to be able to describe and evaluate Freud's psychodynamic explanation of the personality (id, ego, superego), the importance of the unconscious, and catharsis

Freud suggested that there are three aspects to the personality, the id, ego and superego. The **id** is the part of the personality that is present from birth. It consists of our instincts and desires. As the id wants instant wish fulfilment, it is said to operate on the pleasure principle. From birth onwards, the **ego** develops. The job of this part of the personality is to balance the demands of the id and superego. For this reason, it is said to operate on the reality principle. The **superego** is the part of the personality that develops at around age 6. It represents our conscience and is said to operate on the morality principle.

The ego sometimes finds it difficult to respond to the id's drives whilst balancing the demands of the superego. As a result, it may repress unacceptable thoughts in the unconscious mind. The unconscious is the part of the mind that we cannot access. It holds hidden fears, anxieties and conflicts that our ego had difficulties dealing with. For example, an attraction to our best friend's boyfriend or girlfriend may be hidden in our unconscious to stop us feeling guilty.

Aggression is one of our drives. Freud believed that we all have a death instinct (thanatos), which is the desire to go back to before being born and a life instinct (eros), which is the desire to live. Aggression allows us to release frustration and move forward with life. Freud believed that frustration can occur when we can't get something that we desire or when we can't avoid pain. We may show aggression when our id is frustrated by the demands of our superego.

Catharsis refers to the release of emotions such as aggression. Psychodynamic theorists argue that pent up aggression can be released through watching violent TV or playing violent computer games. Playing sport may also release aggression and can be cathartic.

Evaluation:

Studies-Research suggests that when people react in an aggressive way to a frustrating situation, although they may experience less tension at first, it makes them more aggressive later. This contradicts the concept of catharsis. Verona and Sullivan (2008) found that participants who were allowed to press a 'shock' button after being annoyed by a confederate, had a reduced heart rate at first compared to a participants who pressed a 'non-shock' button but then they displayed more aggression later to a blast of hot air. Research by Bandura has found that watching aggressive media can make children more aggressive not less, which contradicts the idea of catharsis.

Explanation-The idea that we can experience aggression as a result of unmet desires has face validity.

Application to real life-Psychoanalysis is a therapy that has developed out of Freud's ideas about unconscious conflicts. This therapy has been used to help people with mental health problems.

You need to be able to compare the biological explanation of aggression with the psychodynamic explanation of aggression

Both the psychodynamic and biological approaches look at how internal factors are involved in aggression. The psychodynamic approach says that aggression occurs due to internal drives and unconscious conflicts whereas the biological approach says that aggression occurs due internal structures such as the amygdala.

There is more scientific evidence for biological explanation of aggression than the psychodynamic explanation. Brain scans such as PET and MRI scans provide evidence for certain physical structures being involved in aggression. In contrast, the psychodynamic approach based its theories on evidence from case studies of unique people. These case studies are not generalisable to the wider population.

Some biological evidence supports the psychodynamic approach. Brain scans show that the limbic system is involved in emotions and aggression. This relates to Freud's theory that our unconscious desires are related to aggression.

You need to be able to describe and evaluate the role of hormones (e.g. testosterone) to explain human behaviour such as aggression

Description:

Hormones are chemical substances that are produced by glands in the body. They travel in the blood to target organs. They are similar to neurotransmitters in terms of carrying messages but they move more slowly. For example, the adrenal glands produce the hormone adrenaline, which moves to target organs such as the heart. Heart rate increases to prepare the body for fight or flight. The testes produce the hormone testosterone, which moves to the male reproductive organs and is needed to produce sperm. It also causes changes at puberty in males such as facial hair, a deep voice and increased aggression. Males often have raised testosterone levels, when aggressive behaviour is shown. Animals that have been injected with testosterone show increased aggression and animals that have had their testes removed display decreased aggression. This supports the link between testosterone and aggression.

Evaluation:

Studies- Brook et al (2001) conducted a meta-analysis of 45 studies and found a mean correlation of + 0.14 between testosterone and aggression. However, much of the research is correlational and cannot establish cause and effect. On the other hand, Bain et al (1987) found no significant differences in testosterone levels in men convicted of violent compared to men convicted of non-violent crimes. Kreuz and Rose (1972) also found no difference in testosterone levels in a group of 21 prisoners who had been classified as violent and non-violent.

Explanation-It is difficult to establish whether testosterone is directly linked to aggression. Higher levels of testosterone may be related to dominant behaviour rather than aggression.

Application to real life-If testosterone levels are linked to violent behaviour, then this has implications for the way we treat violent offenders.

You need to be able to describe and evaluate whether case studies of brain-damaged patients can be used to explain individual differences in behaviour

Description:

Phineas Gage was a railway worker who ended up with an iron rod through his head as a result of an explosion. The rod went through the top of his head and out of the left frontal lobe of his brain. Prior to the accident, he was a quiet, polite man but after the accident he became rude and aggressive. This case study suggests that aggression may be linked to frontal lobe.

Evaluation:

We need to be careful about generalising from case studies of unique individuals to the wider population. The effect of damage to the frontal lobe in Phineas Gage may not be the same in other people.

You need to be able to describe correlational research in psychology. You need to be able to describe types of correlation: positive, negative and including the use of scatter diagrams.

Correlational studies look for a relationship between two variables (called co-variables). For example, it may look for a relationship between the number of hours of violent TV watched and levels of aggression. An example of a positive correlation is: the more hours of violent TV watched, the more aggressive people are. An example of a negative correlation is: the more hours of violent computer games played, the less helpful people are.

Positive correlations occur when two variables rise together. An example would be the higher the happiness rating, the longer the relationship.

Negative correlations occur when one variable rises and the other falls. For example, the higher the age, the lower the number of items recalled from a list.

A correlation coefficient refers to a number between -1 and +1 and states how strong a correlation is. If the number is close to +1 then there is a positive correlation. If the number is close to -1 then there is a negative correlation. If the number is close to 0 then the variables are uncorrelated. For example, +0.9 refers to a strong positive correlation, 0 is no correlation and -0.2 is a weak negative correlation.

Evaluation:

Correlational studies can demonstrate a relationship between two variables, which was not noticed before. They can also be used to look for relationships between variables that cannot be investigated by other means. For example, researchers can look to see whether there is a relationship between parents having low expectations of their children and the children's later academic performance. Manipulating such variables would be unethical. However, correlational studies cannot establish cause and effect relationships. A third factor may affect both variables under investigation. For example, although a correlational study might show a relationship between the number of hours of violent TV watched and levels of aggression, we cannot be certain that the violent TV programmes led to the aggression. It may be that children who watch violent TV programmes are naturally more aggressive and so seek such programmes out.

Scatter diagrams can be used to display data from correlational studies.

A positive correlation

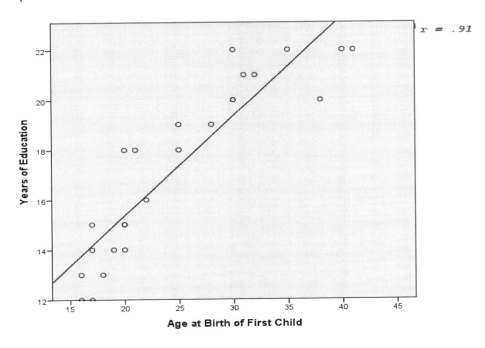

A negative correlation

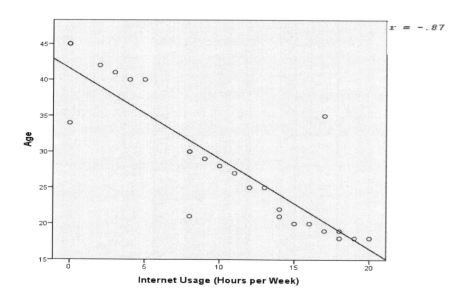

No correlation

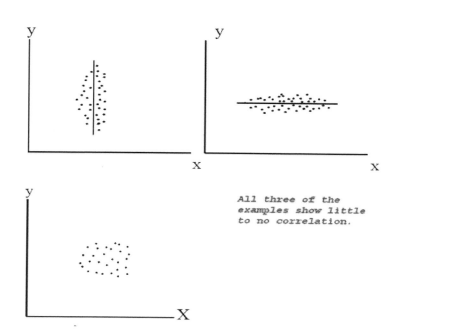

All three of the examples show little to no correlation.

You need to be able to understand the use of alternate, experimental and null hypotheses

An experimental hypothesis predicts what change(s) will take place in the dependent variable (DV) when the independent variable (IV) is manipulated in an experiment.

A two-tailed (non-directional) hypothesis predicts that there will be a change in the DV when the IV is manipulated.
e.g. There will be a difference in the number of words recalled when words are processed semantically compared to when they are processed phonetically.

A one-tailed (directional) hypothesis predicts in which direction the change will take place.
e.g. There will be more words recalled when they are processed semantically compared to when they are processed phonetically.

The null hypothesis states that there will be no changes due to the manipulation of the IV.
e.g.There will be no difference in the number of words recalled when processed semantically or phonetically.

Operationalisation: A hypothesis is operationalised when it is clear what is being manipulated and what is being measured. The dependent variable should refer to a numerical value. For example, if you are measuring recall, you might say number of words recalled.

The term 'alternative hypothesis' is used when predicting what will happen for a study that is not an experiment, for example, a correlational study.
A non-directional (two-tailed) alternative hypothesis predicts that there will be a relationship between two variables. For example, there will be a relationship between the hours of computer games played and empathy scores.
A directional (one-tailed) alternative hypothesis for a correlation would predict whether there will be a positive or negative relationship between two variables. For example, the more hours of computer games played, the lower the score for empathy.
Null hypothesis: There will be no relationship between the number of hours of computer games played and empathy scores.

You need to understand the use of control group

It is important to have a control group in an experiment to compare the experimental group against. For example, if you want to measure the effectiveness of a treatment on a group of patients, you should give a control group a placebo treatment and compare the effects. If you want to measure the effects of giving a cue on memory on a group of participants, then you should have a control group who do not receive a cue.

You need to understand the use random assignment

In order to ensure that the experimental and control groups in a psychology experiment are chosen without bias, random assignment is used. This means that each participant has an equal chance of being assigned to a particular group. Researchers may draw names out of a hat, pick straws or use a computer system to randomly decide which participants are placed in a certain group.

You need to be able to give reasons for using the Spearman's Rho statistical test (A2 knowledge)

Spearman's Rho is used when you have a correlational design and the level of data is ordinal.

The observed value needs to be higher than the critical value for the null hypothesis to be rejected (i.e. to accept the alternative hypothesis).

You need to be able to describe and evaluate the following brain-scanning techniques: CAT, PET and fMRI

CAT (Computerised Axial Tomography) scans

CAT scans use x-rays to produce a series of pictures showing slices of tissue in the brain. The pictures can then be combined to build up a 3D image of the brain. CAT scans can highlight brain damage or the position of tumours in the brain.

Evaluation: CAT scans are easy to carry out and can give accurate images of the brain although they are unable to show brain activity. X-rays can be harmful so CAT scans are only done when there are clear benefits.

Positron emission tomography (PET)

PET scans can be used to produce 3D computer-generated images of the brain. A radioactive substance, called a tracer, is injected into the bloodstream and travels to the brain. As the tracer breaks down it releases energy waves called gamma rays, which are picked up by the PET scanner. More active areas of the brain break down the radioactive substance more quickly. Areas of high activity in the brain produce more gamma rays and this is shown up in red and yellow on the 3D computer image. Areas of low activity are shown in blue and darker colours on the 3D computer image. Psychologists can use PET scanning to find out which parts of the brain are active when performing certain tasks such as a language or spatial task. Raine et al. used PET scans to compare the brain activity of murderers and non-murderers.

Evaluation: PET scans are able to highlight areas of brain activity and can be used to identify parts of the brain that are not functioning normally. However, they require a patient to be injected with a radioactive substance, which although low risk could have potentially harmful effects if done too many times.

fMRI (Functional Magnetic Resonance Imaging)

More active areas of the brain use more oxygen. Our blood carries oxygen so when a specific part of the brain is active, blood flow increases to that area. fMRI works by detecting changes in blood oxygenation and flow in order to measure brain activity. fMRI scans have been used to investigate learning, emotion and memory.

The fMRI scanner is able to detect changes in blood oxygenation and flow because it contains a powerful electromagnet. The magnetic properties of blood differ depending on whether it is oxygenated or deoxygenated. More active areas of the brain receive more oxygenated blood. The fMRI scanner picks up on this.

Evaluation: fMRI scans are useful at showing brain activity when a person is asked to carry out different tasks. They are also non-invasive and do not involve injecting someone with a radioactive substance or exposing them to potentially harmful x-rays. On the other hand, as a strong magnetic field is used, people with pacemakers or metal implants cannot have fMRI scans. Some people can also find the scanners claustrophobic.

You need to be able to describe and evaluate the use of brain scanning techniques to investigate human behaviour e.g. aggression

Bufkin and Luttrell (2005) reviewed 17 neuroimaging studies and found that the prefrontal and medial temporal regions are associated with aggressive behaviour and impulsive acts. Evaluation:

Brain scans might show that certain aggressive traits correlate with a particular brain area but they cannot prove causation. It may be that a third factor is involved such as drug abuse or brain trauma. Furthermore, many brain areas involved in aggression have multiple functions.

You need to be able to describe and evaluate twin studies and give an example of one.

Description:

MZ twins are compared to each other to see whether they share the same characteristics. Concordance rates are used to see the similarity between the twins for a certain characteristic such as IQ, personality or mental disorder. For example, Gottesman (1991) found that if one MZ twin has schizophrenia, there is a 48% chance (0.48 concordance) that the other twin will have it too.
In a twin study, DZ twins are also compared to each other to see what the concordance rates are for certain characteristics in them. For example, Gottesman found that if one DZ twin has schizophrenia, there is a 17% chance (0.17 concordance) that the other one will have it too.
MZ twins share 100% of their genes whereas DZ twins only share 50% of their genes. Therefore, if MZ twins have a higher concordance rate than DZ twins for a certain characteristic such as schizophrenia, this suggests that genes are important in determining this characteristic.

Evaluation:

An assumption with twin studies is that MZ twins and DZ twins share similar environments and the only difference between MZ twins and DZ twins is that MZ twins share 100% of their genes whereas DZ twins share 50% of their genes. However, this assumption can be questioned. MZ twins are often treated more similarly than DZ twins, for example, they are often dressed the same and people may respond to them in similar ways because they look the same. Therefore, it may be the more similar experiences of MZ twins rather than genes, which leads to them having higher concordance rates for IQ, personality characteristics and mental disorders. Studying separated twins make it easier to assess the influence of genes versus environment. However, separated twins may still have shared the same environment for a certain amount of time before separation. Another problem with twin studies is that most people are not twins so it is hard to generalise from twins to the wider population.

An example of a twin study is Lacourse et al. (2014)

Description:

Aim-To see whether genetic factors affect physical aggression in young children.
Procedure-Researchers used 254 MZ twins and 413 DZ twins born between 1995 and 1998 who were part of the Quebec Newborn Twin Study. Mothers were asked to rate their twins on physical aggression at 20,32 and 50 months using a questionnaire with a three point scale – 0 = never; 1 = sometimes; 3 = often for frequency of: hitting / biting / kicking; fighting and attacking another person.
Results-The correlation between MZ twins for physical aggression was 0.7 compared to 0.4 for DZ twins.
Conclusion-Genes play an important role in children's physical aggression.

Evaluation:

Generalisability-The study looked at twins so the findings are difficult to generalise to non-twins.

Reliability-The children were rated for aggression by their mothers only so the study lacks inter-rater reliability.

Application to real life-The study helps us to understand the role of genes in aggression and could be used to identify those children at risk of aggression.

Validity-The mothers of MZ twins may have rated their children with more similar levels of aggression than mothers of DZ twins.

Ethics-Asking mothers to rate their children for aggression could potentially cause problems in their relationships with their children.

You need to be able to describe and evaluate adoption studies and give an example of one.

Description:

Children who have been adopted are compared to their biological parents and adoptive parents for a certain characteristic. If there is greater similarity between the child and their biological parents, this suggests that genes are important for this characteristic. Heston found that 10% of adopted children whose biological mothers had schizophrenia went on to develop it themselves compared to none in the control group. Heston's study suggests a genetic basis for schizophrenia.

Evaluation:

A problem with adoption studies is that adoption agencies usually try to place children in families that are similar to the biological family. Therefore, it is difficult to separate out the influence of genes and the environment. Furthermore, most people are not adopted so it is hard to generalise findings from adoptees to the wider population.

An example of an adoption study: Mednick et al. (2008)

Description:

Aim-To see whether there is an effect of genes on criminality amongst adoptees.

Procedure-14,427 people who had been adopted between 1924 and 1947 in Denmark were studied. The court conviction histories of the adoptees, their biological mothers and fathers and their adoptive mothers and fathers were examined. The researchers used the court convictions to determine the individual's criminal involvement and the occupation was used to determine the person's socioeconomic status.

Results-If neither the biological or adoptive parents of the adoptee had a criminal conviction, then only 13.5% of the adoptees had a conviction themselves. If the adoptive parents had a conviction but the biological parents did not, then 14.7% of the adoptees had a conviction. In contrast, if the biological parents had a conviction, 20% of the adoptees had a conviction. The rate of convictions amongst male adoptees whose biological parents had three or more convictions, was three times that of those adoptees whose biological parents did not have a criminal conviction.

Conclusion-Genes do play a role in criminality.

Evaluation:

Generalisability-It is hard to generalise from adoptees to the wider population as most people are not adopted.

Reliability-Criminal convictions are an objective measure of criminality and this makes the study more replicable and reliable. Cloninger and Gottesman (1987) carried out a similar study and found similar results. This suggests that the findings of this study are reliable.

Application to real life-If genes predispose certain individuals to criminality, then those at risk can be identified and preventative measures can be used.

Validity-It can be hard to separate out the effects of genes and environment. Mednick points out that the biological mothers of the adoptees may not have given their developing baby an ideal environment in the womb, which may have made them more susceptible to criminality.

Ethics-Looking at the court convictions of adoptees and their families may be seen as intrusion on privacy.

Note: Genes are units of information that pass on genetic traits such as personality and intelligence from parents to offspring. 50% of our genes come from our mother and 50% of our genes come from our father. Genes are found in our chromosomes. Chromosomes consist of long strands of DNA (deoxyribonucleic acid).

You need to understand that the biological approach mainly supports the nature side of the nature-nurture debate

The biological approach mainly supports the nature side of the debate. It says that we are born with certain genes and a nervous system that affect the way we think, feel and behave. However, the biological approach accepts that our environment, for example, our diet can affect our development.

Note: The learning approach mainly supports the nurture side of the nature-nurture debate. It says that most of our behaviour is learnt from our environment through operant conditioning, classical conditioning and social learning theory. However, it accepts that we are born with some natural behaviours such as automatic reflexes.

The psychodynamic approach supports the nature and nurture side of debate. It supports the nature side of the debate because it says we are born with certain drives and instincts. On the other hand, it supports the nurture side of the debate because it says our experiences in childhood, our environment, affect us later in life.

You need to be able to describe and evaluate the classic study: Raine et al. (1997) 'Brain abnormalities in murderers indicated by positron emission tomography'

Description:

Aim-To see if murderers who plead not guilty by reason of insanity (NGRI) have localised brain impairments.

Procedure-The experimental group consisted of 41 people (39 men and 2 women) who had been charged with murder or manslaughter in California, USA and were in custody.

They were chosen because they had reasons for pleading not guilty by reason of insanity (NGRI). Reasons included schizophrenia, head injury, substance abuse and learning disabilities. They were matched with a control group of non-murderers based on age and sex. All the participants were asked to carry out a task whilst in a PET scanner.

Results-The PET scans showed that the 41 murderers had lower activity in the prefrontal cortex, parietal cortex and corpus callosum than the non-murderers. They also had higher activity in the occipital lobe. In addition, there were abnormal imbalances of activity in the amygdala, thalamus and medial temporal gyrus including the hippocampus.

Conclusion-Brain dysfunction may predispose a person to violence. Damage to the prefrontal cortex is associated with impulsivity, loss of self-control and the inability to modify behaviour. An imbalance of activity in the amygdala , thalamus and hippocampus could lead to increased aggression.

Note: The sample consisted of people who had been charged with murder and manslaughter but they are all called murderers for ease of reference in this study.

Evaluation:

Generalisability-The study only looked at brain differences in NGRIs so it is difficult to generalise the findings to other types of violent offenders.

Reliability-The researchers tried to control many of the variables. For example, the murderers were carefully matched with a control group based on age and sex. In addition, a PET scan was carried out on all the participants, which is a scientific and objective way of measuring brain activity. This means that the study is replicable and can be tested for reliability.

Application to real life-The study has important implications for the type of sentencing given to NGRIs and to what degree they are responsible for their actions.

Validity-The researchers made inferences from the brain scans and so the results need to be treated with caution.

The PET scan involved participants carrying out a task that had no relation to violence so it is difficult to generalise brain activity during the task to brain activity during a violent act. This questions the validity of the findings.

It is also difficult to establish cause and effect in this study. Although differences in brain activity were found between the murderers and the non-murderers, we cannot be certain that the murderers had these differences before they carried out the murder. It is possible that changes in brain activity occurred as a consequence of carrying out their crime. Furthermore, environmental factors such as a poor home life may have led to the differences in brain activity and the violent behaviour.

Ethics- The research is socially sensitive because it suggests that violent behaviour is biologically determined.

You need to be able to describe and evaluate one contemporary study. For example, Brendgen et al. (2005) 'Examining genetic and environmental effects on social aggression: A study of 6-year-old twins'

Description:

Aim-To look at the relationship between genetic and environmental factors on social and physical aggression.

Procedure-234 six-year old Canadian twins were used from an ongoing longitudinal study (Quebec Newborn Twin Study). Teachers rated the children's levels of physical and social aggression using questionnaires. Indicators of social aggression were the extent to which the children might try to socially exclude another child or spread rumours. The social aggression questions included: to what extent the child 'tries to make other dislike a child', 'becomes friends with another child for revenge' and 'says bad things or spreads nasty rumours about another child'. The physical aggression questions included: to what extent 'the child gets into fights', 'physically attacks others' and 'hits, bites or kicks others'. Responses were given on a 3-point scale (5 never, 15 sometimes, 25 often). For each child, a total social aggression score and total physical aggression score were calculated. Peer ratings of the children's social and physical aggression were also obtained. This was carried out by giving booklets of photographs of all the children in particular class to them. The children were then asked to circle the faces of children who fitted a certain characteristic. The two behavioural descriptors for social aggression were 'tells others not to play with a child' and 'tells mean secrets about another child'. The two behavioural descriptors for physical aggression were 'gets into fights' and 'hits, bites or kicks others'. The total number of nominations for social and physical aggression were then calculated for the twins in the classes. Taking into account different class sizes, a total score for social and physical aggression was worked out.

Results-According to teachers, boys were more physically aggressive than girls but girls were more socially aggressive than boys. However, according to peer ratings, boys were more physically and more socially aggressive than girls. The correlation between the teacher and peer ratings were moderate for physical and social aggression.
The correlations for physical aggression in the MZ twins were almost twice as high as the DZ twins. This suggests that genetic factors play an important role in physical aggression. In contrast, the correlations for social aggression were similar in MZ and DZ twins, which suggests that environmental factors play a greater role in social aggression than genetic factors.

Conclusion-50% to 60% of individual differences in physical aggression in related to genes and the rest to environmental factors. Social aggression is more influenced by environmental factors.

Evaluation:

Generalisability-The study focused on twins, who are not representative of the wider population. It also focused on a specific age group and other age groups may demonstrate their aggression differently. For example, older children may display more social aggression and less physical aggression.

Reliability-The teachers rated the children using a questionnaire with a 3-point scale. The children rated their peers by circling photos of children from a booklet that fitted behavioural descriptions. Therefore, the procedure is replicable and can be tested for reliability.

Application to real life- The study suggests that it is important to target and reduce physical aggression in young children as this can help prevent the development of social aggression later on.

Validity-The study used teacher and peer ratings, which gives the findings greater validity especially as there was moderate concordance between the ratings for social and physical aggression for both groups.

Ethics-Asking children to rate their peers on physical and social aggression could potentially cause conflict between the children.

An alternative contemporary study is: Li et al. (2013) 'Abnormal function of the posterior cingulate cortex in heroin addicted users during resting state and drug-cue stimulation task'

Description:

Aim-To see whether the activation of the posterior cingulate cortex (PCC) of heroin addicts is different to non-addicts when shown drug-related images. To investigate the connectivity between the PCC and different areas of the brain linked to addiction such as the bilateral insula and the bilateral dorsal striatum.

Procedure-14 male detoxed, chronic heroin users were matched with 15 healthy participants based on age and gender. Both groups were giving an fMRI scan when resting. They were also given an fMRI scan during a cue-related task. This task involved 48 pictures, half of which were related to heroin and half of which were neutral. The participants' cravings were measured before and after the images.

Results-There was a significant difference in brain activity between the two groups. The activation of the PCC was greater in the heroin users compared to the non-addicts when shown the heroin-related images. The connectivity between the PCC and bilateral insula and bilateral dorsal striatum was greater in the heroin users as well. The correlation between activity in the PCC and bilateral insula was $r=0.60$. The correlation between activity in the PCC and the bilateral dorsal stratum was $r=0.58$.

Conclusion-The brains of heroin addicts respond differently to heroin-related images compared to non-addicts. Heroin-related images can trigger activity in the PCC and other brain areas linked to rewards and cravings in heroin addicts.

Note: The PCC is involved in autobiographical memories and what we pay attention to emotionally. Therefore, if drug addicts looks at heroin-related images, this may trigger their memories of the heroin use and the emotional cravings.

The bilateral insula is related to our emotions in social situations.

The bilateral dorsal striatum is a critical part of the dopamine reward system, which is activated when people take drugs such as heroin.

Evaluation:

Generalisability-It is hard to generalise from this small, all male sample to the wider population.

Reliability-The heroin addicts were well-matched with a control group of healthy participants, which makes the study more reliable. The fMRI scans measured brain activity in the resting state and when the participants were shown various images under controlled conditions, which makes the study more replicable and reliable.

Application to real life-Understanding how drug addicts' brains respond to drug-related cues could help in their treatment. Recovering drug addicts should be encouraged to avoid any cues that might trigger their desire for the drugs.

Validity-fMRI has been shown to be a good technique for measuring brain activity, which makes the study more valid.

Ethics-The heroin addicts were shown heroin related images and this might have triggered a desire to use the drug, which is unethical.

You need to be able to describe one key question in the biological approach. For example, 'What are the implications for society if aggression is found to be caused by nature not nurture?'

If a person is born to be aggressive due to their genes, hormones, neurotransmitters, brain structure or central nervous system then it could be argued that they don't have a choice in behaving aggressively. This has implications for society. On the other hand, if a person's environment and experiences affect whether they are aggressive or not, then it could be argued that they have a choice whether to behave aggressively or not. A person who has learnt aggression from their environment can also unlearn that behaviour or avoid situations that cause it. In contrast, if aggression stems from biological factors, it is harder to change and it could be argued that people should not be blamed or punished for it. Being criminalised or put in prison for behaviour that is outside a person's control could be considered unfair and unethical.
Applications of concepts and ideas

Brendgen et al. (2005) found that 50% to 60% of individual differences in physical aggression related to genes. This study suggests that certain individuals may be predisposed to showing aggression.

Raine et al. (1997) found differences in brain activity between murderers and non-murderers. Brain dysfunction may predispose a person to violence. Damage to the prefrontal cortex is associated with impulsivity, loss of self-control and the inability to modify behaviour. An imbalance of activity in the amygdala, thalamus and hippocampus could lead to increased aggression.

Phineas Gage was a railway worker whose brain was damaged in a railway accident. After the accident, he became much more aggressive. This suggests that certain parts of the brain are linked to aggression. However, this is a unique study and it is difficult to generalise the findings.

Bard (1940) lesioned the brains of cats and found that the hypothalamus and amygdala were responsible for aggression. However, there are problems with generalising animal research to humans as humans are more complex. For example, the prefrontal cortex in animals is smaller than in humans.

Swantje et al. (2012) found that women with smaller amygdalas were more likely to have higher aggression scores. This supports the idea that the amygdala plays an important role in aggression.

We may have evolved to show aggression. For example, aggressive behaviour may have been an important behaviour in ensuring our survival amongst our ancestors so these traits are more likely to be passed down the generations. Females may have selected males who were more aggressive to provide greater protection for them and their offspring. Male aggression may have been driven by the desire to find a suitable partner. Buss and Shackleton (1997) found that men would try to intimidate other males if they felt their relationship was threatened. This supports the idea that men may use aggression to maintain their relationships with women and to ensure their genes are passed on.

Brook et al (2001) conducted a meta-analysis of 45 studies and found a mean correlation of + 0.14 between testosterone and aggression. However, much of the research is correlational and cannot establish cause and effect. Higher levels of testosterone may be related to dominant behaviour rather than aggression.

McDermott et al. (2009) found that people with a particular version of the MAOA gene (the 'warrior gene'), which shows low activity were more likely to be aggressive and impulsive especially if they have high levels of testosterone too.

Research which show that aggression is linked to differences in genes, brain functioning or hormones suggest that people who display aggression may not be in control of their behaviour and so cannot be blamed for it. If a person's biology is leading to their aggressive behaviour, then a key question is should they be criminalised or punished for it?

You need to be able to describe a practical you carried out in the biological approach. Example practical: To see whether there is a correlation between brain sex and aggression

Aim: To see whether there is a correlation between brain sex and aggression

Alternative directional hypothesis: The higher the male brain score, the high the aggression score.

Null hypothesis: There will be no relationship between male brain score and aggression score.

Procedure: Participants were briefed about the aims of the study and what they would be asked to do at the beginning. An opportunity sample of 10 female participants between 16-17 years old was used. They were asked to complete an online quiz on brain sex in a silent computer room. Their percentage score for having a male brain was recorded. They were then asked to complete a questionnaire which measures aggression levels. Participants were asked to note down their aggression scores and male brain scores on a sheet of paper without their name on and to fold it to be collected in to ensure anonymity. A Spearman's rho statistical test was carried out on the data to see whether there was a relationship between the male brain score and aggression score. Participants were debriefed at the end. They were given the right to withdraw throughout.

Results:

Participant number	Male brain score (A)	Aggression score (B)	Rank A	Rank B	d=Rank A-Rank B	d^2
1	56	66	9	4	5	25
2	75	70	3	2	1	1
3	45	40	10	10	0	0
4	71	60	4	7	3	9
5	62	65	6	5	1	1
6	64	56	5	9	4	16
7	58	59	8	8	0	0
8	80	77	1	1	0	0
9	76	67	2	3	1	1
10	61	63	7	6	1	1

d=the difference between the ranks
d^2= the difference between the ranks squared

The formula for Spearman's rho is:

$$r_s = 1 - \frac{6\sum d^2}{n(n^2 - 1)}$$

Step 1: Work out the sum of d^2. Note the symbol, $\sum$, means 'sum of'.

$\sum d^2 = 25+1+9+1+16+1+1=54$

Step 2: We then substitute this into the main equation with the other information. Remember n=10 as there were 10 participants.
$r^s = 1 - 6 \sum d_i^2/n\,(n^2-1)$
$r^s = 1 - 6 \times 54/10(10^2-1)$
$r^s = 1 - (324/990)$
$r^s = 1 - 0.33$
$r^s = 0.67$

The r^s value of 0.67 indicates a strong positive relationship between the male brain score and aggression. That is, the higher you ranked for male brain score, the higher you ranked in aggression.

Note: The Spearman correlation coefficient, r_s, can take values from +1 to -1. A r_s of +1 indicates a perfect positive correlation, a r_s of zero indicates no relationship and a r_s of -1 indicates a perfect negative correlation. The closer r_s is to zero, the weaker the relationship between the co-variables.

You need to be able to compare the observed value of r^s with the critical value. To find the critical value in a critical values table, you need to look for n=10 as there were 10 participants and $p \leq 0.05$. For Spearman's rho, the observed value of r^s need to be bigger than the critical value for the result to be significant.

Conclusion: There is a relationship between male brain score and aggression score.

Evaluation:

Generalisability-An opportunity sample of 10 female students was used. As only females were used, the sample is not representative of the wider population.

Reliability-As questionnaires were used to measure brain sex and aggression, it is possible to replicate the procedure. This makes the study more reliable. However, on a different day, participants might have answered the questions differently.

Application to real life-Understanding how brain sex affects aggression, could lead to greater understanding of the causes of aggressive behaviour.

Validity-The online brain sex quiz may have lacked validity. The questions asked may not have been a true reflection of brain sex. The questionnaire measuring aggression may not have reflected real life aggression and participants may have given socially desirable answers. Correlational studies cannot establish cause and effect relationships. There may be other factors involved affecting both co-variables.

Ethics-Participants may have felt distressed if they scored highly for aggression and may have felt uncomfortable writing their scores down.

Exemplar Exam Question

A 9-year-old boy gets into a fight with his friends at school and his mother says, 'Boys will be boys'.

Discuss the role of hormones in aggression with reference to the statement 'boys will be boys'.

Student Answer:

Testosterone is produced in the testes and is needed to produce sperm and leads to male secondary sex characteristics such as facial hair and a deep voice. At puberty, when testosterone levels rise in males, aggression often increases. Furthermore, there is a rise in testosterone levels, when men display aggression. This provides support for the theory that testosterone relates to aggression. However, it is difficult to know whether testosterone leads to aggression or whether aggression produces higher testosterone levels.

Animals that have been injected with testosterone show increased aggression and animals that have had their testes removed display decreased aggression. This supports the link between testosterone and aggression.

Many correlational studies have found a relationship between testosterone and aggression. However, much of the research is correlational and cannot establish cause and effect. There is also conflicting evidence. Bain et al (1987) found no significant differences in testosterone levels in men convicted of violent crimes compared to men convicted of non-violent crimes. Kreuz and Rose (1972) also found no difference in testosterone levels in violent and non-violent offenders. Higher levels of testosterone may be related to dominant behaviour rather than aggression.

Testosterone has been shown to influence levels of the neurotransmitter serotonin, which is linked to mood. Low levels of serotonin are linked with aggression. Therefore, testosterone may have an indirect effect on aggression by modulating serotonin levels.

9/12 marks

Commentary:

This student has covered a wide range of points related to hormone levels and aggression. However, they have not related it to the comment, 'boys will be boys'. It is important to relate your answer to the scenario given in the exam. For example, this student could have said that boys have higher testosterone levels than girls and as testosterone is linked with aggression this may have led to the comment 'boys will be boys'.

Chapter 4-Learning Theories

You need to be able describe what the learning approach is about

The learning approach focuses on how our behaviour is influenced by the environment. It makes the following assumptions: we respond to stimuli in our environment and behaviour is affected by our experiences.

You need to be able to describe and evaluate classical conditioning

Description:

Classical conditioning refers to the process of learning through association. When a neutral stimulus is paired with an unconditioned stimulus, we can become 'conditioned' to respond to the neutral stimulus. The neutral stimulus becomes a conditioned stimulus and produces a conditioned response.

E.G. Pavlov's dog study
Food (UCS) $\longrightarrow$ Salivation (UCR)
Food (UCS) + Bell (NS) $\longrightarrow$ Salivation (UCR)
Bell (CS) $\longrightarrow$ Salivation (CR)

Extinction: When a conditioned response is suppressed. This occurs when the conditioned stimulus is no longer paired with the unconditioned stimulus. For example, if a dog is no longer given food (unconditioned stimulus) when it hears a bell (conditioned stimulus), it will stop salivating (conditioned response) to the sound of the bell. Extinction does not mean that the behaviour has been unlearnt; it just means that the behaviour has become dormant.

Spontaneous recovery: A conditioned response may be dormant but suddenly reappear again. For example, a dog's conditioned response of salivating to a bell may extinguish but then reappear later when the dog hears the sound of a bell.

Stimulus Generalisation is when someone becomes conditioned to respond to not only the conditioned stimulus but also similar stimuli. For example, Little Albert became conditioned to not only fear white rats but also other white furry objects.

Note:

A stimulus is something that causes a response. For example, a spider might be a stimulus that causes a fear response.

A response is a reaction to a specific stimulus. For example, salivation might be the response to the stimulus of food.

Evaluation:

Studies-Watson and Rayner's Little Albert study showed how a baby could learn to fear a white rat through classical conditioning. This study supports the idea that behaviours can be learnt through association.

Pavlov's study on dogs showed that dogs would learn to salivate to the sound of a bell through the association of food and a bell. This study supports the idea that behaviours can be learnt through association.

Explanation-Classical conditioning is reductionist because it focuses on how behaviour is learnt through association and does not take into account other factors involved in behaviour e.g. genes and social factors.

Note: Reductionist means reducing behaviour down to one thing and not taking into account other factors.

Application to real life-Classical conditioning can explain how we learn phobias and other behaviours through association. For example, it can explain why dogs get excited when their owners get their leads out because they have associated it with going for a walk.

You need to be able to describe and evaluate Pavlov (1927) experiment with salivation in dogs

Description:

Aim-To investigate digestion in dogs by measuring the amount of saliva produced by a dog when it eats. (Pavlov had not aimed to investigate classical conditioning)

Procedure-Meat powder was placed directly on the dog's tongue or in a bowl. A tube was surgically attached to the dog's cheek near one of the salivary glands and a fistula was made so that the saliva drained straight out into a measuring device. Pavlov measured the amount of saliva that occurred naturally whenever food was placed in the dog's mouth as salivation is an involuntary, reflex response.

Results-He observed that the dogs salivated not only at the sight of the food, but also at the sight or sound of the laboratory technician who had been preparing the food.

Conclusion-He concluded that salivation is a natural, reflexive response to food and that this involuntary response can become associated with a neutral stimulus such as the laboratory technician.

Further experiments: Pavlov was intrigued by these unintentional observations and carried out further experiments. He conducted a study to see whether a dog would salivate to the sound of a bell if it had become associated with food.

UCS (Food) → UCR (Salivation)
NS (Bell) + UCS (Food) → UCR(Salivation)
CS (Bell) → CR (Salivation)

An UCS (unconditioned stimulus) is something that naturally causes you to respond in some way.

An UCR (an unconditioned response) is a natural, involuntary response. For example, salivating to food is a reflexive response.

A NS (a neutral response) is a stimulus that you feel neutral towards (it can becomes a CS)

A CS (a conditioned stimulus) is something that you would <u>not</u> normally respond to but since being paired with an UCS makes you respond in a certain way

A CR (a conditioned response) is learnt response that has occurred as a result of classical conditioning. For example, salivating to the sound of a bell is not a natural response but a learnt/ programmed response.

Evaluation:

Generalisability-Humans have more complex cognitive (thinking) capacities than animals so it is hard to generalise the research to humans. However, numerous studies have since found that classical conditioning occurs in humans as well as animals.

Reliability-Pavlov carried out a standardised procedure that he replicated with different dogs to test for reliability. He used a number of different stimuli to see whether he could create an association and found the same results, which shows the study is reliable. He controlled the extraneous variables to find out the causes of the dogs 'salivation and this ensured he had established a cause and effect relationship.

Application to real life-The study can explain many learnt behaviours. For example, dogs get excited when their owners get their leads out because they have associated this with going for a walk.

Validity-The study was carried out in an artificial setting of a laboratory so it lacks ecological validity. However, because the study was carried out on dogs, it could be argued that they would have responded naturally irrespective of the artificial environment. The dogs displayed natural, involuntary responses to the stimuli, which are valid.

Ethics-Pavlov surgically altered the dogs so that he could collect their saliva outside of their bodies. This caused physical harm to the dogs. The dogs were strapped/tied down during the experiments, which would have caused them distress.

You need to be able to describe and evaluate Watson and Rayner (1920) 'Little Albert: Conditioned emotional reactions'

Description:

Aim-To see whether Little Albert could be classically conditioned to be afraid of a stimulus he was originally unafraid of.

Procedure-Little Albert was chosen for the study because he was an emotionally stable child who was not easily frightened. He was also familiar with the hospital environment as his mother worked there. At 9 months old, he was tested to see whether he was afraid of a variety of stimuli. He was unafraid of a white rat but was afraid of the sound of a metal bar being banged. When Albert was 11 months old, the researchers decided to classically condition him to be afraid of a white rat. Albert was shown the white rat and when he reached out to touch it, a loud noise was made with a metal bar behind his head. This was repeated several times.

UCS (banging of bar) $\longrightarrow$ UCR (Fear)

UCS(banging of bar) + NS(rat) $\longrightarrow$ UCR(fear)

CS (rat) $\longrightarrow$ CR (fear)

Originally the rat is a neutral stimulus (NS) but once it begins to cause fear, it becomes a conditioned stimulus (CS)

Results-Little Albert showed a fear response to the rat on its own after a number of pairings of the rat and the banging bar over a period of a week. At 11 months 15 days old, Little Albert was happy to play with some toy blocks but showed fear towards the rat. He also showed a negative response to a rabbit and a fur coat suggesting he had transferred his fear of the white rat onto similar objects.

Conclusion-This study showed that Little Albert was classically conditioned to be afraid of a stimulus he was originally unafraid of. It also showed that conditioned responses can be generalised to other similar objects.

Evaluation:

Generalisability-The study was carried out on only one boy so it is hard to generalise it to the wider population.

Reliability-This laboratory experiment had good controls and a procedure that would be easy to replicate. The researchers carefully observed and recorded Little Albert's responses to the stimuli, which makes it reliable. They also made sure Little Albert was not afraid of furry things and rats before the study. However, if the study was repeated with other children, it may be difficult to replicate the findings as other children might be afraid of a white rat but unafraid of a banging metal bar.

Application to real life-This study can explain how humans learn phobias through association. For example, a child may be initially afraid of spiders but unafraid of going into a shed. However, they may become afraid of the shed after a spider runs across their shoe in the shed.

Validity-The study lacks ecological validity because it was an artificial situation. In real life, stimuli are not carefully paired together under controlled conditions as the white rat and banging bar were in this study.

Ethics- Little Albert was not protected from psychological harm. He was only 11 months old when he took part in the experiments and he was caused distress. For example, he showed fear and cried when shown the white rat. They also did not extinguish his fear.

You need to be able to describe how phobias may occur through classical conditioning

Anxiety and fear can become associated with neutral stimuli leading to anxiety disorders and phobias. For example, you might observe someone being mugged on a certain street and afterwards have a phobia of walking down this street.

UCS (Mugging) → UCR (Fear)
NS (Street) + UCS (Mugging) → UCR(Fear)
CS (Street) → CR (Fear)

You need to be able to describe and evaluate treatments for phobias based on classical conditioning principles: flooding and systematic sensitisation

Systematic desensitisation description:

Systematic desensitisation is based on classical conditioning principles. It can be used to get rid of phobias. There are four processes in systematic desensitisation: functional analysis, constructing an anxiety hierarchy, relaxation techniques and gradual exposure. Functional analysis involves discussing triggers for the phobia with the therapist. The therapist and client then construct an anxiety hierarchy. The idea is to help a person overcome their phobia by starting with something less fearful and working up to the real fear. For example, a student with a fear of attending school might have a picture of their school at the bottom of their anxiety hierarchy. One step up their hierarchy might be driving past their school. Next it might be going into the school playground and finally at the top of the hierarchy would be going into a classroom. The third process in systematic desensitisation is teaching the client relaxation techniques such as deep breathing and visualising being in a safe comfortable place. The final process is gradual exposure. The client moves up their anxiety hierarchy at their own pace using relaxation techniques at each stage. The person learns to associate being relaxed with their feared stimulus instead of fear response. For example, the student begins to associate school with feeling relaxed rather than feeling anxious.

Evaluation:

Directive-The therapist guides the treatment but the patient has a lot of control over the treatment. They only progress up the hierarchy when they feel confident enough. Therefore, the treatment can be considered less directive and more ethical.

Effectiveness-Systematic desensitisation helps people get over phobias especially of animals and objects. The positive effects seem to last for longer than some other therapies.

Side effects-None. It is less stressful than flooding.

Expense-It can take a long time for the patient to make progress in overcoming their phobia. Therefore, systematic desensitisation can be expensive in terms of both time and money.

Reasons-Systematic desensitisation does not look at the underlying causes of a phobia. For example, a person may suffer from a certain phobia due to a traumatic experience, which is not addressed during the therapy.

Types of people-Systematic desensitisation tends to be better for people with phobias of animals or objects rather than those with social phobias.

Flooding description:

Flooding is a therapy used to get rid of phobias. It is based on the principles of classical conditioning. During the therapy, patients are forced to confront the object or situation that is causing them distress and they are not allowed to escape. For example, a person with a fear of heights might be taken up to the top of a very tall building and told to stay there until their distress diminishes. The idea is that continued exposure to the feared stimulus weakens and extinguishes the fear as the initial anxiety cannot be sustained.

Evaluation:

Directive-During flooding, the therapist forces the patient to confront their phobia and may even stop them running away. The therapist therefore has a lot of control over the treatment and it can be viewed a directive.

Effectiveness-Wolpe (1973) used flooding to help a young woman overcome her phobia of cars. She was made to sit in the back of a car and was driven around continuously for four hours. Initially she was hysterical with fear but the fear response eventually subsided. This study supports flooding as a technique for overcoming phobias.

Side effects-Flooding can cause patients to become very distressed, which raises ethical issues. Some people may find the approach too difficult and withdraw from the therapy before it's finished. This could lead to the fear or phobia becoming worse.

Expense-Flooding can work quickly, and therefore, it is cheaper than systematic desensitisation in terms of both time and money.

Reasons-Flooding does not look at the underlying causes of a phobia. For example, a person may suffer from a certain phobia due to a traumatic experience, which is not addressed during the therapy.

Types of people-Flooding works by getting people to confront a feared stimulus so it is helpful for people with a fear of objects or animals. However, it is less useful for people with less concrete fears such as fear of failure. Flooding works better on people who are motivated to change and prepared to experience highly stressful situations.

You need to be able to describe and evaluate operant conditioning

Operant conditioning refers to the process of learning through consequences: Positive reinforcement (rewards), negative reinforcement (removing something unpleasant) and punishment (providing something nasty or removing something nice).

Positive reinforcement refers to giving a reward for a desired behaviour. For example, a dog might be given a treat for sitting down when their owner says 'sit'. Behaviour that is positively reinforced is more likely to be repeated.

Negative reinforcement refers to taking away something unpleasant for a desired behaviour. For example, a teacher might take away homework for particularly good work in class. Behaviour that is negatively reinforced is more likely to be repeated.

Positive punishment refers to giving a nasty consequence (such as a detention) for an undesired behaviour. For example, a child might be told to sit on the naughty step for pinching another child. Behaviour that is positively punished is less likely to be repeated.

Negative punishment refers to taking away something nice for an undesired behaviour. For example, a parent might take away a child's toy for bad behaviour. Behaviour that in negatively punished is less likely to be repeated.

Note: Reinforcement increases the frequency of desired behaviours. Punishment decreases the frequency of undesired behaviours. Reinforcement and punishment can be both positive and negative. Think positive (+) means adding or giving something and negative (-) means taking away or removing something.

Primary reinforcers are rewards that satisfy a basic need, such as food, drink, warmth and shelter. Fizzy drinks, sweets, chocolate and cake are all types of primary reinforcer.

Secondary reinforcers are rewards that are not fulfilling on their own but can be exchanged for something that satisfies a basic need. Secondary reinforcers are only fulfilling because they are associated with a primary reinforcer e.g. money can be used to buy food. Merits, tokens and vouchers are types of secondary reinforcers.

Shaping is when a behaviour is learnt by rewarding moves towards the desired behaviour (successive approximations of the desired behaviour). First of all behaviour that is on the way to the desired behaviour is rewarded and then later on only behaviours that are nearer and nearer to the desired behaviour are rewarded. For example, shaping helps children acquire language. When a child first vocalises, their parents are delighted and give the child lots of attention and praise. The attention is rewarding and so the child repeats vocalisations. The parents then begin to only praise (positively reinforce) vocalisations sounding like words so the child begins to only repeat word sounds. Later the parents only reinforce the child when they produce real words so that word sounds (e.g. gadad) are shaped into words (e.g. granddad).

Evaluation:

Studies-Skinner found that rats would press a lever to receive a reward. This supports operant conditioning as it shows how behaviour can be learnt through consequences. However, this study is not generalizable to humans as humans are more complex. For example, humans have language and can adapt their behaviour based on what they are told rather than just through consequences.

Explanation-Operant conditioning is useful at explaining how behaviours such as addictions and language are learnt through consequences. However, it is reductionist because it focuses on learning through consequences and does not take into account other factors.

Application to real life-Token economy programmes are based on operant conditioning. Operant conditioning principles can be applied to help children behave better through rewards and punishment. Language acquisition can be explained through shaping.

You need to be able to describe different schedules of reinforcement and their effects on learning: continuous reinforcement; fixed interval; variable interval; fixed ratio and variable ratio

There are different ways to arrange the delivery of reinforcement/rewards: Continuous reinforcement and partial/intermittent reinforcement.

Continuous reinforcement is when every desired behaviour is reinforced/rewarded. It is useful when you are trying to teach a new behaviour. However, behaviour that is continuously reinforced can become extinct quickly if the reinforcement is no longer given. Furthermore, if the same reward is given all the time, then there is a risk of reinforcer satiation (the reward is no longer desired so the behaviour may no longer be performed).
Intermittent reinforcement is when some, but not all, desired behaviours are rewarded. Behaviour that is only intermittently reinforced is more resistant to extinction and so intermittent schedules of reinforcement are useful in maintaining established behaviours. There is also less risk of reinforcer satiation with an intermittent schedule.

There are different types of intermittent reinforcement schedules: fixed ratio (FR), fixed interval (FI), variable ratio (VR) and variable interval (VI).

Ratio schedules are based on giving reinforcement after a certain number of desired behaviours.

Fixed ratio (FR) schedules involve reinforcement being given after a set number of responses/behaviours. For example, you might give a reward every fourth time a child tidies their toys up (FR-4). Fixed ratio schedules result in a high rate of desired responses but it can lead to a drop in the desired behaviour straight after the reinforcement is given. Another problem with fixed ratio schedules is that if a person has to wait too long for reinforcement, they might stop performing the desired behaviour. Therefore, if you are changing from a continuous reinforcement schedule and moving to a fixed ratio schedule, you should reinforce behaviour quite frequently. For example, you might start by offering a reward every two behaviours and move up to offering a reward every four behaviours and so on.

Variable ratio (VR) schedules involve reinforcement being given after a varying number of responses. For example, with a VR-6 schedule, rewards are given on average every six desired behaviours but reinforcement might come after three behaviours one time, after nine behaviours another time and after six behaviours the time after that. Variable ratio schedules are good at encouraging desired behaviour long-term with no post-reinforcement pauses. As reinforcement can occur at any time, extinction is not likely. It is possible to move from a continuous reinforcement schedule to a low reinforcement variable ratio schedule easily.

Interval schedules involve reinforcement being given for desired behaviour after a certain amount of time has elapsed.

Fixed interval (FI) schedules involve reinforcement being given for desired behaviour after a set amount of time has passed. For example with a FI-2 minute schedule, reinforcement is given after 2 minutes if the behaviour has already occurred or as soon as the behaviour occurs after the 2 minutes has elapsed. For example, you might try to use a fixed interval schedule to get your child to stay seated at dinner time. After 2 minutes, if your child has not got out of their seat yet, you might give them praise or a star on a chart. However, extinction can occur if schedule is thinned too quickly. For example, if you start giving rewards only every 20 minutes too early in the process, then the desired behaviour may become extinct.

Variable interval (VI) schedules involve reinforcement being given for desired behaviour after varying time intervals. For example, with a VI-10 minute schedule, reinforcement is given for the desired behaviour at varying time intervals with an average of 10 minutes. For example, a teacher could set a timer that goes off at varying intervals to encourage the students to stay on task. The timer might go off after 5 minutes, 15 minutes and then 10 minutes (an average of 10 minutes) and the teacher could praise the students if they are on task at these varying intervals. Variable interval schedules have the most resistance to extinction of any schedule. There are also no post-reinforcement pauses, because intervals between reinforcement are not predictable.

You need to be able to describe how some techniques based upon the principles of operant conditioning can be used to modify problem behaviour. For example, Token Economy Programmes

Description:

Token Economy Programmes (TEPs) are used in mental health institutions, schools and prisons to modify problem behaviour. TEPs are based on the principles of operant conditioning. Tokens (secondary reinforcers) are given for desired behaviour and these can then be exchanged for primary reinforcers. For example, in schools a pupil might be rewarded with merits for good behaviour. Once the pupil has a certain number of merits they might be able to exchange them for a book voucher. In prisons, cooperative and non-aggressive behaviour is rewarded. Prisoners may need to collect a certain number of tokens, which they can then exchange for something they actually want such as a phone card (a primary reinforcer). In mental health institutions, patients are rewarded for more adaptive behaviour. For example, anorexic patients are given tokens if they gain a certain amount of weight each week and these tokens can be exchanged for outings.

Evaluation:

Directive: Staff implementing a token economy programme have a lot of power. It is important that staff do not favour or ignore certain individuals if the programme is to work. Therefore, staff need to be trained to give tokens fairly and consistently even when there are shift changes such as in a prison or in a psychiatric hospital.

Effectiveness- TEPs can quickly change behaviour. Hobbs and Holt found direct short-term success in using TEPs with youth offenders. They recorded the effects of introducing a TEP to youth offenders in three institutions, while a fourth acted as a control. They found the TEP led to a significant increase in the targeted behaviours compared to the group not involved. On the other hand, although TEPs may be effective whilst an offender is in an institution, it may only change behaviour temporarily. Once the offender leaves the prison and goes into the outside world, there may be no real change in thinking or behaviour. Pearson et al. found that behavioural treatments such as TEPs were not good at stopping reoffending. TEPs can be useful with those with mental health issues. TEPs have been useful at getting sufferers of anorexia nervosa to a reasonable weight after which issues can be addressed. TEPs can also be effective with schizophrenics who lack the motivation to perform self-care tasks. Allyon and Azrin (1968) used a TEP to change the behaviour of 45 chronic schizophrenics who had been institutionalised for an average of 16 years. They were given tokens for making their beds or combing their hair. After the TEP, the schizophrenics were much better at looking after themselves.

Side effects- TEPs can lead to learned helplessness where prisoners or patients feel that they have no choice about taking part in the programme. TEPs may also stop people looking inside themselves for the problem.

Expense-TEPs are relatively cheap to implement as staff do not need much training to deliver them. However, staff need to give the rewards and punishments consistently and this can be difficult to achieve especially with shift changes.

Reasons-TEPs do not address the underlying causes of the person's behaviour such as family issues and traumatic experiences.

Types of people-TEPs can be used effectively in institutions such as schools, hospitals and prisons but they may be viewed as patronising by people outside an institution.

You need to be able to describe how phobias can be maintained through operant conditioning

Phobias may be maintained through coping techniques such as avoidance and escape. Avoidance refers to behaviours that attempt to prevent exposure to a fear-provoking stimulus. Escape means to quickly exit a fear-provoking situation. For example, a person who has a phobia of heights may avoid going to high places. This coping strategy rewards them by reducing their feelings of stress and anxiety. Another person may feel uncomfortable in a crowded room, so they leave to reduce their anxiety. Both avoidance and escape are highly reinforcing because they remove or diminish the unpleasant feelings. However, they do not stop the anxiety from re-occurring again and again in the future. So the principles of operant conditioning can explain how a phobia is maintained.

You need to be able to describe and evaluate social learning theory

Social learning refers to learning through observation and imitation. For social learning to occur, the learner must pay **attention** to and **retain** the model's behaviour. The learner must have the physical abilities to **reproduce** the behaviour and the learner must be **motivated** to imitate the behaviour. If the model is rewarded this increases the likelihood that the learner will imitate the behaviour. This is called **vicarious reinforcement**. For example, a girl may observe her older sister bake a cake and get praise for it. She is more likely to copy her sister's behaviour because she has seen her sister be rewarded for it.

Observation with reference to social learning theory refers to watching a model's behaviour. For example, a girl may watch her older sister put on make-up.

Imitation refers to copying a behaviour after it has been modelled. For example, a boy may play with a toy gun in the same way his friend does.

Modelling refers to learning new behaviours by observing other people. The modelling process involves the following processes: attention, retention, reproduction and motivation. For example, a boy may pay attention to his father playing the guitar and retain the behaviour. In order to reproduce the behaviour, he will need to practise the guitar. Finally, to successfully imitate his father's playing ability, he needs to be motivated to copy the behaviour.

Vicarious reinforcement refers to a behaviour being reinforced because another person has been observed receiving a reward for it. For example, a boy is more likely to work hard on his sums at school, after seeing another boy get rewarded with a sticker for completing a set of sums quickly.

Models of the same gender and age are more powerful (are more likely to be imitated). Models of higher status such as celebrities are also more likely to be copied.

Exam tip: Use ARRM to help you describe social learning theory. Attention, Retention, Reproduction and Motivation.

Evaluation:

Studies-Bandura's Bobo doll experiments found that children will copy aggressive behaviour shown by a model. This supports the idea that behaviour can be learnt through observation and imitation.

Explanation-Social learning theory is reductionist because it focuses on how behaviour is learnt through observation and it does not take into account other factors that affect our behaviour e.g. genes. However, social learning theory can explain how our thoughts and motivations affect behaviour. For example, people will have increased motivation to copy high status models who are rewarded for their behaviour. They are also more likely to imitate the behaviours of a role model if they feel confident in their abilities to reproduce the behaviour (self-efficacy).

Application to real life-Modelling-based therapies are based on the principles of social learning theory. Positive role models can be used to encourage people to change their behaviour.

You need to be able to describe and evaluate Bandura, Ross and Ross (1961) original Bobo doll experiment

Description:

Aim-1)To see if children might observe aggressive behaviour and then model their own actions on it. 2) To investigate the impact of gender on modelling.

Procedure- The study involved 72 children from one nursery in the USA. There was an equal mix of boys and girls and they were between 3- to 5-years-old. 24 of the children were put in a control group and did not observe a model at all. The remaining 48 children were divided into eight conditions: Condition 1-Boys watch aggressive, male model; Condition 2-Boys watch non-aggressive male model; Condition 3-Boys watch aggressive, female model; Condition 4-Boys watch non-aggressive female model; Condition 5-Girls watch aggressive, male model; Condition 6-Girls watch non-aggressive male model; Condition 7-Girls watch aggressive, female model and Condition 8-Girls watch non-aggressive, female model.

The children in the different conditions were matched individually on the basis of ratings of their aggressive behaviour in social interactions in the nursery school. During the experiment, the children were taken individually into a room by the experimenter and seated at a table where they could design pictures with potato prints and picture stickers provided. The experimenter then brought the adult model to the opposite corner of the room where there was a tinker toy set, a mallet, and a 5-foot inflated Bobo doll. The experimenter then left the room. Children in the non-aggressive condition saw a model quietly play with some tinker toys in the corner. Children in the aggressive condition, saw the model play with the tinker toys and then after one minute behave aggressively to the Bobo doll. The model sat on the Bobo doll and punched it repeatedly in the nose. The model then raised the Bobo doll, picked up the mallet and struck the doll on the head. The final aggressive act in the sequence was throwing the model into the air and kicking it around the room. The model then repeated this sequence of aggressive acts approximately three times. The model also made verbally aggressive comments such as, "Sock him in the nose . . . ," "Hit him down . . . ," "Throw him in the air . . . ," "Kick him . . . ," "Pow . . . ," and two non-aggressive comments, "He keeps coming back for more" and "He sure is a tough fella."

After 10 minutes, the experimenter entered the room and took the child to a different room to play after saying goodbye to the model. When they got to the new room, the children were all put into a slightly aggressive state by being told that they could not play with certain toys. This was to make sure that all the children were at the same level of aggression. The children were then observed playing. The researchers scored any behaviour to the Bobo doll that was imitative of the specific aggressive acts shown by the model to the Bobo doll.

Results-The children who had watched the aggressive models were more aggressive. In the non-aggressive and control conditions, approximately 70% of the children had a zero score for aggressive acts. Boys were more physically aggressive than girls but there was little difference for verbal aggression. The children were more likely to imitate same sex models. The mean number of aggressive acts committed by the boys was 25.8 after observing the male model and 12.4 after observing the female model. The boys showed more than double the number of aggressive acts towards the Bobo doll after observing a male model compared to a female model.

Conclusion-When children watch adults being aggressive they are likely to imitate that aggression, so it shows that observational learning takes places (social learning theory). Children are more likely to copy same-sex models. Boys, in particular, are more likely to be aggressive after observing a same-sex model be aggressive.

Evaluation:

Generalisability-All the children were from one nursery in the USA so it is hard to generalise from the study to the wider population.

Reliability- The study was a laboratory experiment with good controls so it is replicable and reliable. The researchers matched the children on levels of aggression at start. Inter-observer reliability was established by having more than one observer.

Application to real life-This study suggests that children are likely to copy violence shown by models. Therefore, children's exposure to violent role models in real life, on TV or in computer games should be limited.

Validity-The study involved an artificial situation so it lacks ecological validity. The children who saw the model behave aggressively to the Bobo doll, may have thought that they were supposed to behave that way towards the Bobo doll. If they had seen a model behave aggressively to a real person, they may have been much less likely to copy the behaviour. The children knew that the plastic Bobo doll could not be hurt so the study does not measure real aggression.

Ethics-The children who watched the aggressive model may have been made more aggressive and this is an ethical issue.

Credibility-Although the study showed that children will copy aggressive behaviour shown by a model immediately, it does not establish any link between watching violence and long-term aggressive behaviour.

To be able to describe and evaluate Bandura, Ross and Ross (1963) Bobo Doll experiment

Description:

Aim-To compare imitative behaviours when children watch an aggressive model in the same room as them, on film and using a cartoon character.

Procedure-48 boys and 48 girls from one nursery school in the USA were used. They ranged in age from 35 to 69 months. The children were divided into three experimental groups and one control group with 24 participants in each group. In one experimental group, children watched a real life aggressive model, in the second group, they watched a human model be aggressive in a film and in the third group, they watched an aggressive cartoon character in a film. As in the 1961 study, the children were sub-divided further into male and female participants so that half the children saw same-sex models and half the children saw opposite sex models. The control group saw no aggressive model at all. Participants in the experimental and control groups were matched for aggression on the basis of their social interactions in the nursery school by the experimenter and nursery school teacher. Children who had been assigned to the real life aggression group, were sat at a table at one corner of a room with potato prints, stickers and coloured paper, while an adult model was taken to the opposite corner of the room, which contained a small table and chair, a tinker toy set, a mallet and a 5-foot inflated Bobo doll. The experimenter left and then the model played with the tinker toy set for approximately one minute before behaving aggressively to the Bobo doll. In order, to measure imitative aggression, the model carried out the following distinctive acts of aggression: the model sat on the Bobo doll and punched it repeatedly in the nose, the model raised the Bobo doll and hit it on the head with a mallet and finally the model tossed the Bobo doll up into the air and kicked it about the room. This sequence of aggressive acts was repeated three times. The model also made verbally aggressive comments such as, "Sock him in the nose . . . ," "Hit him down . . . ," "Throw him in the air . . . ," "Kick him . . . ," "Pow . . . ," and two non-aggressive comments, "He keeps coming back for more" and "He sure is a tough fella."

Children in the human-model film group were sat at a table with potato prints and shown a film for 10 minutes with the same models as in the real life aggression condition displaying the same aggressive acts towards the Bobo doll.

Children in the cartoon film group were sat at a table with potato prints, coloured paper and stickers while being shown a film of a female model dressed up as a black cat performing aggressive acts. The cat was similar to many cartoon cats and to make it more like a cartoon, the backdrop was composed of brightly coloured trees, birds and butterflies and there was cartoon music in the background. The cat performed the same aggressive acts to the Bobo doll as the human models had but the movements were done in a more feline way. The same verbally aggressive comments were made but in a high-pitched animated voice.

After the children had seen the aggressive models, the children were brought to an anteroom with a number of attractive toys. They were then told that they couldn't play with these toys but they could play with the toys in the next room. This was to make them all feel equally frustrated and aggressive. They were then brought to an experimental room, which contained a mixture of aggressive and non-aggressive toys. The aggressive toys included a 3-foot Bobo doll, a mallet and two dart guns. The children's behaviour was observed through a one-way mirror for a period of twenty minutes. There was more than one observer to establish inter-observer reliability.

Results-The mean total aggression scores for participants in the real-life, human film, cartoon film and control groups were 83, 92, 99 and 54 respectively. The children who had observed the human models displayed more imitative aggression than those who had seen the cartoon model. However, the children who had observed the cartoon model demonstrated many partially-imitative acts such as carrying out the aggression towards an object other than the Bobo doll. The children who watched the aggressive models exhibited nearly twice the amount of aggression than children in the control group. The boys performed more imitative aggression than the girls.

Conclusion-Exposure to aggressive human and cartoon models in film and real life increases aggressive behaviour in children.

Evaluation:

Many of the same evaluative points can be made as for Bandura, Ross and Ross' (1961) study.

An additional point that can be made about this study is that it provides further evidence that media violence can lead to aggression. The results suggest that there should be a watershed and films should have ratings.

You need to be able to describe and evaluate Bandura (1965) Bobo doll experiment with vicarious reinforcement

Bandura's (1965) study was different to the original study in three ways: The children observed an adult be aggressive to a Bobo doll on a film rather than in the same room as them; the study looked at vicarious reinforcement and the children were offered rewards (stickers and juice) for each behaviour they copied.

Description:

Aims-To see whether children will copy an aggressive model shown in a film clip. To see whether the model being punished, rewarded or having no consequences for the behaviour affects the children's desire to imitate the aggressive behaviour. To see how many of the aggressive behaviours the child will imitate when given rewards.

Procedure-33 boys and 33 girls aged between 3 and 6 years old were split into to three conditions: Model rewarded; model punished and model receives no consequences. The children watched a film showing an adult be aggressive to a plastic Bobo doll. The film ended in three different ways: The model was rewarded by being praised for their aggressive behaviour; the model was punished by being told off and spanked with a rolled up newspaper and the model experienced no consequences for their aggressive behaviour. After watching the film, the children spent 10 minutes in the same room with a Bobo doll and other toys. Two observers recorded the number of imitative behaviours the children displayed. The children were asked to copy what Rocky did in the film and offered stickers and juice for each physical or verbal response they copied.

Results-The children who saw the model receive rewards or no consequences for the aggressive behaviour were more likely to copy it. The same number of imitative behaviours were shown by these two groups. The children who saw the model punished copied the aggressive behaviours less. When the children were offered rewards for copying, there was no difference between the groups.

Conclusion-Children are less likely to copy a model's behaviour if they see the model punished. However, the children all learnt the behaviours even in the model-punished condition and they were able to copy the behaviour when given rewards for doing so.

Evaluation:

Many of the same points can be made as for the 1961 study.
An additional point is that the children not only watched aggressive behaviour in this study but were also rewarded for aggressive behaviour, which may have made them more aggressive. Therefore, this study is more unethical than the original study.

You need to be able to describe and evaluate one contemporary study. For example, Becker et al. (2002) 'Eating behaviours and attitudes following prolonged exposure to television among ethnic Fijian adolescent girls'

Background:

The researchers were interested in whether increased exposure to television would affect eating behaviours amongst Fijian girls. Fiji was chosen because it has an extremely low prevalence of eating disorders. It had only one reported case of anorexia by the mid- 1990s.The Nadroga province of Fiji was selected because of its lack of exposure to television until mid-1995. Furthermore, Fijian culture encourages robust appetites and larger figures.

Description:

Aim-To look at the impact of the introduction of television on eating behaviour and attitudes in Fijian adolescent girls.

Procedure-A cross-sectional design was used to compare two groups of Fijian girls at secondary school in forms 5-7 before and after prolonged television exposure. The first group of girls were tested in 1995, within weeks of the introduction of television to Nadroga, Fiji. 63 girls took part (mean age 17.3 years). The second group of girls were tested in 1998, after the area had been exposed to television for three years. 65 girls took part (mean age 16.9 years). There was no significant difference between the girls in terms of mean age or body mass index. 41.3% of the sample had television sets in their homes in 1995 compared to 70.8% in 1998. The girls were asked to complete a 26-item eating attitudes test (EAT-26), which included questions on bingeing and purging behaviour. A score greater than 20 was considered high. Girls who self-reported bingeing or purging on the test were asked to respond to a semi-structured interview to confirm their symptoms.

Results-The percentage of participants with EAT-26 scores greater than 20 was 12.6% in 1995 compared with 29.2% in 1998. The percentage of participants reporting self-induced vomiting to control weight was 0% in 1995 compared to 11.3% in 1998. Respondents living in a household with a television set were three times as likely to have a EAT-26 score greater than 20. 74% of the 1998 group reported feeling 'too big or too fat' at least some of the time. 62% of the 1998 group reported dieting in the four weeks prior to the study and 77% reported that television had influenced their own body image. In 1998, they frequently said during the interviews that they wanted to lose weight or reshape their bodies to be more like a Western Television characters.

Conclusion-This study suggests that television can have a negative impact on eating attitudes and behaviours.

Evaluation:

Generalisability-It is hard to generalise from Fijians to other cultures. The marked disparity between normal Fijian body shapes and the slender figures shown on TV may make Fijians particularly vulnerable to developing eating disorders due exposure to TV images. Fijians may also associate thinness with glamour as the characters on TV often have expensive clothing and good careers.

Reliability-The EAT-26 test was replicable. This increases the reliability and objectivity of the study. The interviews would be hard to repeat and are open to interpretation. This makes this element of the study more subjective.

Application to real life-It has helped us to understand how thin media celebrities can be connected to disordered eating attitudes.

Validity-This naturalistic experiment has good ecological validity as it was able to assess the impact of television on a traditional society. Qualitative data was collected via interviews, which gives the study greater validity.

Ethics-Interviewing vulnerable adolescent girls with high EAT-26 scores regarding their eating behaviour may have caused them distress.

Credibility-Scores on the EAT-26 test cannot be equated with a clinical diagnosis of an eating disorder. However, high EAT-26 scores and induced vomiting are associated with eating disorders.

You need to be able to describe and evaluate one key question. For example, 'Is the influence of role models and celebrities something that causes anorexia?'

In our society, images of the female body in magazines, on TV and in films all suggest that being thin is beautiful. These images and thin celebrities in the media act as models for women in our society. There is an argument over whether these images lead to anorexia nervosa or whether anorexia nervosa is caused by other factors such as genes or family issues.

Social learning theory suggests anorexia nervosa may be due to role models in the media. Young people may feel they have to get to around the same weight as thin celebrities in order to be accepted. Teenagers pay attention to the fact that many celebrity role models are extremely thin and are likely to retain this information. They have the ability to reproduce being thin if they diet excessively and will do it if they are motivated to do so. They can see that their role models are famous and rich and this may motivate them to be thin too. Teenagers may also think that they need to be thin in order to be accepted by their peers, which may also provide motivation for excessive dieting.

Evaluation:

There are a number of studies which support social learning theory as an explanation of anorexia nervosa. Becker et al. (2002) found that the women living on the island of Fiji started developing eating disorder symptoms after the introduction of Western TV channels. Nasser (1986) compared Egyptian women studying in Cairo with similar Egyptian women studying in London and found that 12% of those living in London developed eating disorder symptoms, compared to 0% in Cairo. Lai (2000) found that the rate of anorexia increased for Chinese residents in Hong Kong as the culture slowly became more westernised. Mumford et al. (1991) found that Arab and Asian women were more likely to develop eating disorders if they moved to the West. These studies suggest that it is Western media images that lead girls and women to diet excessively and develop eating disorders. However, Eysenck and Flanagan (2000) point out that although all young women in the West are exposed to the media, only 3-4% of them develop an eating disorder. Therefore, there must be other factors other than media images that play a role in the development of anorexia.

Social learning theory cannot explain why anorexia nervosa usually develops in adolescence. A psychodynamic explanation for anorexia nervosa is that the disorder develops due to fears about growing up. Family issues may also contribute to the development of anorexia. Parents of anorexics may be too controlling and not allow their child to explain their own needs. Some anorexic sufferers report that they started dieting as method of gaining control over their lives. Genetics may also predispose someone to anorexia as the disorder does run in families. Relatives of people with eating disorders are four or five times more likely to also suffer (Strober and Humphrey, 1987).

You need to be able to describe how phobias can be learnt through social learning theory

Phobias can be learnt through observation and imitation. For example, a young boy may develop a phobia of spiders because his father has one. The young boy pays attention to the fact that his father shows signs of fear in the presence of spiders. He remembers this behaviour and because he views his father as a role model and wants to be like him, the next time he sees a spider he may copy his father's behaviour. In this way, the boy may develop a phobia of spiders.

You need to be able to describe and evaluate observations

There are structured laboratory observations and naturalistic observations. Structured laboratory observations involve careful controls and a set-up situation that can be repeated. There is often more than one observer and observations tend to be carried out through a one-way mirror to avoid the researchers' presence affecting participants' behaviour. Naturalistic observations involve observing participants in their natural environment. For example, observing children's behaviour in a playground.

Observations can be overt or covert. Covert observations involve observing a person or group of people without their knowledge. Overt observations involve observing a person or group of people with their knowledge.

Observations can also be participant or non-participant. A participant observation involves the researcher interacting with the person or group of people that they are observing. A non-participant observation involves the researcher observing behaviour from a distance without having any influence or getting involved.

An observation can be carried out by counting the frequency of certain behaviours during a fixed period of time.
Event sampling-when you record every time an event such as a kick occurs
Time sampling-when you record what is happening every set amount of time e.g. every 5 minutes.
Point sampling- The behaviour of just one individual in the group at a time is recorded.
Inter-observer reliability-Comparing the ratings of a number of observers as an individual observer may be biased.This would increase the reliability of the data collected if all the observers agree.

Evaluation:

Researchers may find it difficult to record all the behaviours shown, although event sampling, time sampling and point sampling can help. Video recordings can be used to record participants' behaviour and played back later so that all actions can be noted. It may also be difficult to analyse or interpret all the data collected. Observers often have to be specially trained so that they can record behaviours quickly and to avoid bias.

Participant observations allow researchers to experience the same environment as their participants. However, the researcher's involvement can affect the behaviour of participants. In contrast, non-participant observations allow researchers to observe participants' behaviour more objectively as they are not directly involved in the action. However, if participants are aware they are being observed, they may still change their behaviour.

Covert observations enable researchers to observe participants behave naturally as the participants do not know they are being observed. However, there are ethical issues with observing participants without their consent. They do not have the right to withdraw, they have not given informed consent and there also issues of confidentiality especially if their behaviour has been video-recorded. The British Psychological Society advises that it is only suitable to conduct a covert observation in a place where people might reasonably be expected to be observed by other people such as a shopping centre or other public place. Overt observations do not have as many ethical issues as covert observations. However, when participants know they are being observed they may change their behaviour so that it appears socially desirable. Therefore, overt observations can be less valid.

You need to be able to describe and evaluate the laboratory experiment as a research method

The learning approach uses laboratory experiments with both animal and human participants.

A laboratory experiment involves manipulating an independent variable to see the effect on a dependent variable. The dependent variable is measured. The extraneous variables are controlled in order to establish a cause and effect relationship.

For example, in Bandura, Ross and Ross (1961), the researchers manipulated whether the children saw an aggressive model, a non-aggressive model or no model at all. They then measured the number of aggressive behaviours shown by the children. This meant that they collected quantitative data, which could be statistically analysed to see how significant the results were.

Evaluation:

Laboratory experiments have standardised procedures, which are easy to replicate so that reliability can be tested. Data from laboratory experiments is quantitative and objective. Due to the careful manipulation and control of variables in a laboratory

109

experiment, a cause and effect relationship can be established. Such evidence is considered scientific.

However, laboratory experiments lack ecological validity because they take place in artificial environments and often involve artificial tasks. Participants may behave unnaturally in an artificial situation. Experimenter effects can also affect laboratory experiments. The characteristics of the researcher may affect participants' responses. Furthermore, demand characteristics can affect results. Participants may guess what the study is about and give responses that they think the researcher wants.

You need to be able to describe, evaluate and carry out a content analysis

A content analysis involves changing qualitative data into quantitative data. This often means tallying how many times certain themes occur within a source such as a newspaper article, magazine article, journal article, radio programme or television programme. The source may be coded or broken down into manageable categories, for example, by words, phrases, sentences or themes. The researcher then analyses the presence and meaning of these categories and draws conclusions. For example, a researcher might tally how often negative or positive comments about daycare occur within two newspaper articles and draw conclusions about how daycare is portrayed in the media.

Evaluation:

As the data comes from secondary sources such as newspaper articles or television programmes, it does not change. Therefore, other researchers can check whether any conclusions are correct or not. The quantitative tallying of themes allows the data to be statistically analysed. There are unlikely to be any ethical issues with a content analysis, as it only involves analysing existing sources. However, the categorising and tallying of themes in a content analysis can be subjective.

You need to be able to describe and evaluate the use of animals in psychological research

Animal studies involve studying animal behaviour either in a laboratory or in the field. In an experiment, an independent variable is manipulated and a dependent variable is measured.

Example of laboratory experiments using animals

Skinner wanted to see whether he could get rats to learn behaviours through the principles of operant conditioning. He placed rats in a special cage called a Skinner's box to investigate their behaviour. He found that the rats would learn to press a lever every time they saw a flashing light in order to receive a reward. The flashing light acted as an antecedent (A=Antecedent), the rat's response/behaviour would be to press the lever (B = Behaviour) and the consequence would be that the rat received food (C = Consequences). Skinner called this the ABC of operant conditioning.

Evaluation:

Advantages: Animals are easier to use than humans because of ethical issues. Animals are also smaller on average, which makes certain experiments easier to run. For example, Skinner needed a small animal for his Skinner's box. Some animals such as rats breed quickly, which means that you can see how selective breeding affects behaviour. For example, if you breed rats that are good at finding their way around mazes together, then you can see whether their offspring are particularly good at mazes.

Disadvantages: Humans are more complex than animals and so it is difficult to generalise results from animal studies to humans. There can be ethical issues with carrying out studies on animals.

You need to be able to discuss ethical guidelines in relation to animals (non-human participants)

Caging and Stress: Experimenters should avoid or minimise stress and suffering for all living animals. The cages the animals are kept in during the experiment should be large enough for the animals to be comfortable.

Number or animals used: Researchers should use as few animals as possible.

Wild Animals: Endangered species should not be used, unless the research has direct benefits for that species e.g. conservation.

Qualified Experimenters: The researchers conducting the experiment should have the necessary qualifications. They should also have a licence from the Home office for that particular experiment.

Look for alternatives: Alternatives to using animals must always be sought, such as using humans or computers.

You need to be able to describe the Bateson's cube

Bateson's cube has three labelled sides: quality of research, animal suffering and certainty of medical benefit. These are on a scale high to low. When a research proposal falls into the opaque region, the experiment should not be conducted i.e. when quality of research is low, animal suffering is high and certainty of benefit is low.

You need to know when to use the chi-square test and how to compare the observed and critical values to judge significance

A chi-square test is a test of difference or association. For example, if males and females tend to choose different types of cars we could say that there is a difference between the genders in terms of car choice or an association between gender and car choice. The chi-square test is used when the data level is nominal, there is an independent measures design and when you are looking for an difference between two groups. There must be a minimum of 5 scores in each category, to carry out a chi-squared test.

The experimental or alternative hypothesis should state that there will be a difference between the two groups. An example of a one tailed (directional) hypothesis is: More males will drive large cars than females.

The null hypothesis should state that there is difference between the groups e.g. There will be no difference between males and females in terms of size of car driven.

For a chi-square test, if the observed value is greater than the critical value shown in a table, then the null hypothesis can be rejected.

The formula for the chi-squared test is:

$$\chi^2 = \sum \frac{(O-E)^2}{E}$$

O = the frequencies observed

E = the frequencies expected

$\sum$ *= the 'sum of'*

For example, a researcher might want to show that more males drive large cars than females and they might collect the following data:

	Male	Female	Totals
Car judged large	19	10	29
Car judged small	6	15	21
Totals	25	25	50

First work out the degrees of freedom (df) for this contingency table:

df= (rows-1) x (columns-1)= (2-1) x (2-1) = 1 x1= 1

A table can then be used to help in the process of working out the chi-square value:

O	E	O-E	$(O-E)^2$	$(O-E)^2/E$
19	14.5	4.5	20.25	1.40
10	14.5	-4.5	20.25	1.40
6	10.5	-4.5	20.25	1.93
15	10.5	4.5	20.25	1.93
				=6.65

The calculated value of chi-square is 6.65. This is called the observed value because it has been obtained from the data observed by the researcher.

Note:
O= observed frequencies. This refers to the number of males and females driving large cars and small cars observed by the researcher.
E=expected frequencies. This refers to what the researcher might expect to see if there is no association between gender and size of car driven. For example, if 29 large cars were observed. You would expect half of them to be driven by females and half of them to be driven by males. 29/2=14.5. Therefore the expected frequency is 14.5.

In order to find out if the observed value of 6.65 is significant or not, it must be compared to the critical value. You need to find the correct critical value in a critical values table for chi-square. Make sure you look for the critical value that corresponds for df=1 and $p \leq 0.05$ for a one-tailed hypothesis. This is 2.71.

As observed value of 6.65 is bigger than the critical value of 2.71, we would say that the result is significant and more males do drive large cars than females.

You need to be able to discuss the scientific status of psychology including: replicability, reliability, validity (internal, predictive and ecological), reductionism, falsification, empiricism, hypothesis testing and use of controls

Scientific knowledge is built from testing theories and collecting empirical data. Empirical data is data gathered through our senses. For example, we might time how long it takes males to complete a spatial awareness task versus females. This is empirical data. Empiricism is the theory that experience is of primary importance in giving us knowledge of the world. John Locke said our mind is a tabula rasa, a "blank slate", when we enter the world. At birth we know nothing but then we learn about the world through our senses and experiences.

Scientific research usually follows a hypothetico-deductive model. A researcher may come up with a hypothesis (prediction) based on a theory. For example, the theory of cue-dependent forgetting might lead to the hypothesis: participants will recall more words with a cue than without a cue. The hypothesis is then tested to see whether it is supported by empirical evidence. Based on the evidence collected, the theory is rejected or accepted.

A key concept in science is falsifiability, which refers to whether a theory can actually be tested or not. The concept of schema in the cognitive approach cannot be falsified so it is considered unscientific. However, the concept of short-term memory can be falsified so it is scientific.

Reductionism refers to reducing a theory into parts. This makes it easier to test. For example, the theory of operant conditioning can be broken down into parts, which can be tested. Skinner tested this: Animals were more likely to repeat a behaviour if they were given a reward and less likely to repeat it if they were punished.
The opposite of reductionism is holism. This means looking at a person as a whole rather than in parts. For example, it may be better to look at a range of factors affecting gender behaviour rather than just focusing on biological reasons. However, this is harder to test scientifically.

For research to be considered scientific, other people need to be able to replicate the study and find the same results. If the same or similar results are found, this suggests the study is reliable.

A scientific study should control any extraneous variables that could affect the results. It is important to establish that it is the independent variable that is leading to a change in the dependent variable rather than any other extraneous variables. For example, in Skinner's study on rats the independent variable was whether the rats were given a reward or punishment for pressing a lever and the dependent variable was the repetition of the behaviour. This was done under controlled conditions so that a cause and effect relationship could be established between the independent variable and the dependent variable.

For a study to have internal validity as few of the following must affect results: Extraneous variables; attrition (participants dropping out before the end of the study); non-random assignment; demand characteristics and experimenter effects. Avoiding these problems makes the study more scientific.

Laboratory experiments tend to be more scientific but they can lack ecological validity.

A study has predictive validity if it accurately predicts a result in the future. CATs tests has predictive validity if they predict accurately that those who score highly on the tests, will go on to get good grades at GCSE. A study or test that has predictive validity is more scientific.

The learning approach is considered to be scientific because it uses laboratory experiments with good controls to investigate how behaviour is learnt.

You need to be able to describe an observation you carried out. Example practical: An observation of how gender affects polite behaviour

Background: Social learning theory suggests that learn gender appropriate behaviour through copying same-sex role models. Women in our society are expected to behave in a polite way in public. Younger females may observe their behaviour and then model this behaviour.

Aim: To see whether gender affects polite behaviour.

Independent variable: Gender

Dependent variable: Whether the person thanks the café assistant or not.

Directional hypothesis: More females will thank the café assistant than males.

Design: Independent groups design as two groups: males and females.

Ethical issues: The study can be considered ethical because the participants were observed in a public place and only their gender and whether they thanked the café assistant were recorded.

Procedure: The observation was carried out on in the sixth form café and care was taken so that students did not think they were being observed (so that their behaviour was not affected by the observation at all). Data was gathered by discreetly tallying the number of thank yous given by male and female students on a mobile whilst sat in the café near the serving area. Qualitative data was collected by noting down when a male or female made conversation with the café assistant and what was actually said in shorthand. The amount of eye contact was also added to the notes.

Participants: There were 20 participants altogether. Their age ranged from 16- to 18-years-old.

Results:

Quantitative data

	Male	Female	Totals
Thanked the café assistant	12	16	28
Did not thank the café assistant	18	7	25
Totals	30	23	53

More females (16) said 'Thank you' than males (12). More males (18) did not say 'Thank you' than females (7).

The observed value was 4.567 which is greater than the critical value of 2.71 (for df=1 and $p \leq 0.05$) so the results are significant. The null hypothesis can be must be rejected.

Note: A chi-squared test was carried out on the results as the study used an independent groups design and the level of measurement was nominal. The critical value was taken from a table of critical values for the chi-squared test. 2.71 is the critical value for df=1 and $p \leq 0.05$ for a one-tailed hypothesis.

Qualitative data

The male students made more conversation with the café assistants. They were more likely make a joke or ask them about their day than the female students. The female students made more eye contact with the café assistants and were more likely to give a simple 'Thank you' when they received their food or drink.

Conclusions:

There was a significant difference in the gender of the student and whether they said thank you to the café assistants. Female students were more likely to say 'Thank you' than male students. However, male students were more likely to talk to the café assistants. Females are more polite than males but males are friendlier.

Evaluation:

Validity: This study took place in participants' natural environment so it has ecological validity. Participants were observed buying food and drink in an everyday situation of a sixth form cafe. Counting the number of times the students said 'Thank you' was an objective measure of politeness, which increases validity. The qualitative data collected from the conversations is subject to interpretation.

Reliability: It would be difficult to replicate the findings of this study as it took place in participants' natural environment and there were no controls over extraneous variables. Results were collected in the middle of day and results might have been very different in the early morning when students might be have been more tired and less likely to engage in conversation. If the study was replicated in a café in a different school or town, findings might be different. Having more than one observer could have improved reliability. If there is a high level of agreement between the observers, then the study can be said to have inter-rater reliability.

Generalisability: The participants may not be representative of the wider population as only sixth form students were used.

Credibility: The study has credibility because it was a naturalistic observation of students in an everyday situation.

Exemplar Exam Questions

Polly has a fear of cotton wool. At university, she will have to share a bathroom with other students. She knows that she needs to overcome her phobia of cotton wool and is deciding between systematic desensitisation and flooding.

Describe how systematic desensitisation and flooding could be used for Polly's phobia. Evaluate the therapies and discuss the things she should consider before choosing between the therapies. (12 marks)

Student Answer:

Systematic desensitisation is based on classical conditioning principles and it can be used to get rid of phobias. It involves helping someone to gradually face up to their fears. During systematic desensitisation, Polly would first discuss her phobia of cotton wool and the triggers with a therapist. Together they could create a hierarchy of anxiety. At the bottom of the hierarchy might be looking at a picture of some cotton wool, then it might be sitting in the same room as some cotton wool, then it might be having the cotton wool on the same seat and finally it might involve touching some cotton wool. Polly can decide the pace at which she'd like to progress up the hierarchy. This will all be made a lot easier by the therapist as they will teach her relaxation techniques to deal with her phobia. She will use these techniques while gradually moving up the anxiety hierarchy.

Flooding is also based on classical conditioning principles. It would involve exposing

Polly to cotton wool for a long period of time without letting her escape from the situation. The idea is that Polly's anxiety will reach a peak and then come back down again. She will then realise that the cotton wool is not going to cause any harm to her.

When deciding between flooding and systematic desensitisation, Polly would need to decide how quickly she wants the therapy to work and what degree of stress she is willing to undergo. Systematic desensitisation takes longer than flooding as it is a gradual process of relaxation and moving up the anxiety hierarchy. However, flooding is more stressful than systematic desensitisation as Polly would not be able to escape from the feared stimulus of the cotton wool.

8/12

Commentary:
This student has described systematic desensitisation and flooding well. However, they could have identified the four processes in systematic desensitisation more clearly: functional analysis, developing an anxiety hierarchy, relaxation training and gradual exposure. They should have also spent more time evaluating the therapies. For example, McGrath et al. (1990) found that systematic desensitisation was effective with 75% of people with phobias. Flooding raises ethical issues as the therapist prevents the client escaping from their feared stimulus and may be viewed as having too much control.

Assess token economies as a form of behaviour modification (8 marks)

There are 4 marks here for demonstrating a knowledge and understanding of the different factors involved in token economies (AO1 marks) and 4 marks for considering the significance of different factors and making a balanced judgement (AO3 marks).

Student Answer:

Token Economy Programmes (TEPs) are useful in institutions such as prisons, schools and mental health units to modify problem behaviour through the principles of operant conditioning. They have been found to quickly control unmanageable behaviour. Hobbs and Holt (1976) found that TEPs significantly improved behaviour amongst young offenders in three institutions compared to a fourth institution, which acted as a control. Whitby & Miller (2009) reported that TEPs can be successful at helping children behave in schools leading to a better learning environment.

On the other hand, TEPs are unlikely to help with the underlying aspects of behaviour. TEPs may be effective with an offender whilst they are in prison but this only changes their behaviour temporarily. Once the offender leaves the prison and goes into the outside world, there may be no real change in thinking or behaviour. Pearson et al. found that behavioural treatments such as TEPs were ineffective at preventing reoffending compared to cognitive behavioural therapies such as anger management, which change thinking. Anorexic patients may gain weight under a TEP in order to be allowed to go on outings and have visits home but it is also important to address their distorted thinking and any family issues otherwise their eating disordered symptoms will continue once they leave the institution.

It is important that rewards are motivating in a TEP and that behaviours are agreed upon in advance for a TEP to be effective. TEPs are relatively cheap to implement as staff do not need much training to deliver them. However, in order for a TEP to be successful, tokens need to be given fairly and consistently even when there are shift changes such as in a prison or in a psychiatric hospital. It is also possible for staff to abuse their power by favouring some offenders or patients over others.

TEPs can lead to learned helplessness where prisoners or patients feel that they have no choice about taking part in the programme. TEPs may also stop people looking inside themselves for the problem.

In conclusion, TEPs can be effective at modifying behaviour in institutions short-term but other methods such as cognitive behavioural therapies need to be used to change behaviour long-term. In order for TEPs to work successfully, rewards have to be given consistently by staff and prisoners/patients have to be motivated by the rewards. TEPs are judged to be effective and useful in institutions at modifying behaviour quickly but not at addressing underlying issues.

8/8 marks

Commentary:
This student demonstrates a good knowledge of token economies whilst assessing their effectiveness. They discuss practical or ethical issues related to it and make comparisons with cognitive behavioural treatments, which involve changing faulty thinking. The final paragraph comes to a conclusion and makes a judgement.

15935397R00067

Printed in Great Britain
by Amazon